DEVELOPING A SUCCESSFUL
SERVICE PLAN

Other titles in the Successful LIS Professional series

THE SUCCESSFUL LIS PROFESSIONAL

SERIES EDITOR
Sheila Pantry

DEVELOPING A SUCCESSFUL
SERVICE PLAN

Sheila Pantry OBE and Peter Griffiths

LIBRARY ASSOCIATION PUBLISHING
LONDON

First published 2000

British Library Cataloguing in Publication Data
A catalogue record for this book is available from the British Library.

ISBN 1-85604-392-4

Typeset in 11/14pt Aldine 721 by Library Association Publishing.
Printed and made in Great Britain by MPG Books Ltd, Bodmin, Cornwall.

Contents

Series Editor's preface

With rapid technological advances and new freedoms, the workplace presents a dynamic and challenging environment. It is just these advances, however, that necessitate a versatile and adaptable workforce which accepts that lifelong full-time jobs are a thing of the past. Work is being contracted out, de-structured organizations are emerging, and different skills and approaches are required from all workers, who must solve new and changing problems. These workers must become self-motivated, multi-skilled and constantly learning. Demonstrating the international economic importance of professional development, the European Commission has officially voiced its support for a European community committed to lifelong learning.

For the information professional, the key to success in this potentially destabilizing context is to develop the new skills the workplace demands. Above all, the LIS professional must actively prioritize a commitment to continuous professional development. The information industry is growing fast and the LIS profession is experiencing very rapid change. This series has been designed to help you manage change by ensuring the growth of your own portfolio of professional skills. By reading these books you will have begun the process of seeing yourself as your own best resource and accepting the rewarding challenge of staying ahead of the game.

The series is very practical, focusing on specific topics relevant to all types of library and information service. Because your time is precious, these books have been written so that they may be easily read and digested. They include instantly applicable ideas and techniques which you can put to the test in your own workplace, helping you to succeed in your job.

The authors have been selected because of their practical experience and enthusiasm for their chosen topic and we hope you will benefit from their advice and guidance. The points for reflection, checklists and summaries are designed to provide stepping stones for you to assess your understanding of the topic as you read.

In *Developing a successful service plan*, Peter Griffiths and I demonstrate why it is vital for you to produce, maintain and continually update your service plan so as to achieve a truly professional service, and at the same time achieve a strategic position for the service in your organization. The book also provides guidance on personal and professional development plans. The books in this series are *intentionally* short in length and are intended to help the busy professional. Although they cannot deal with *all* situations in great detail, there are extensive lists of other information sources to allow the reader to follow up on any point.

We have both drawn on our many previous jobs, and hope that our experiences will be of some help to all LIS professionals, whichever environment they are working in.

May I wish you enjoyment and satisfaction in your endeavours to successfully produce a service plan.

Sheila Pantry, OBE

Foreword

Why this book?

Most successful businesses have a business plan which outlines the nature of the core business, the developments or new products to be offered, the expected performance, and the resources and staff needed to maintain and achieve new business.

This approach ensures that all those involved can participate in the business plan compilation. A service plan is needed for all types of libraries and information centres, irrespective of background or size, and ranging from one-woman/man outfits to larger systems or sections within a system. Research of the literature shows that very little has been written specifically on business planning for the library and information world. Hence this book!

Putting a service plan together requires you to translate your thoughts about how you are going to run the information service. This activity will appeal to all staff, but especially those just starting their careers, or just starting to be involved in planning. In actual fact, planning should include all staff development.

All successful LIS practitioners need to be able to develop services and staff under their control, as well as their own careers, and we show how this can be dovetailed into the service plan.

Most information services/sections need to have an achievable service plan but many staff do not know how to put one together, so we hope that by reading this book you will find out how to start, and see how useful it is to prepare one. Producing such a plan can be exciting because, through talking to all the 'stakeholders' – staff, users, managers in other departments or sections, finance holders, and external organizations – you will become enthused about developing services and systems which are achievable and can be financed successfully.

Producing a service plan can take time, but we show you how you can negotiate the necessary steps and, at the same time, understand the pluses and minuses of having such a plan. You will find that it is also possible to use the service plan process to change attitudes and perceptions.

If a service plan is to be successful it needs to be evaluated and monitored on a continual basis, taking on board customers' requirements and understanding when to introduce new services. Involving others, such as suppliers, is also essential, and you can use your service plan to create a strategic position for the information service in the organization.

We are sure you will find the concept of producing a service plan to be of great benefit, and wish you every success in producing your own successful service plan.

Chapter 1
Why you need a service plan

> **In this chapter you will find:**
>
> ➤ a definition of a service plan
> ➤ the scope of a plan
> ➤ the pluses and minuses of having a plan
> ➤ the use of a service plan to change attitudes and perceptions.

You should think of a service plan as the statement to your users of what the information service (IS) or learning resource centre (LRC) is going to achieve in the forthcoming years. Your plan could span two to three years ahead, but it will need constantly revising (see Chapter 6 for more of this). This goes for all information services – be they academic, special or workplace, public, healthcare, governmental, legal or finance-based.

The first part of the job of an information service is to make sure that the organization (or community, or whatever) realizes that there is no viable alternative to a professional information and library service. (The non-viable alternative is to do without information – a strategy that works fine until the first blunder through lack of information, after which the problem may well disappear when the organization goes out of existence or the community splinters through lack of communication.)

The second part of the job is to ensure that the organization realizes that its information and library services are not simply an overhead cost but can contribute to the bottom line of the balance sheet, certainly in terms of added value and perhaps in hard cash. If more money cannot be voted to the information and library service, then the service should at least show that it is providing more value for every pound, dollar or euro than it did before. An information and library service that can demonstrate this approach has the right to be heard, and respected for its contribution.

Having a service plan which is realistic will enable the information service to contribute to the success of the total organization.

So what is a service plan?

It is the result of a number of actions in which you will be involved on different fronts. It will include:

> what your organization wants to achieve
> the role of the IS in the wider goals of your organization
> the needs of your users
> the development of services provided by the IS
> the enhancement of any technology-based services
> the equipment, materials and acquisitions
> building costs, refurbishment costs
> telecommunication, postal and other costs
> the training and development of IS staff to be able to fulfil user needs and provide enhanced services
> the training of users to be able to benefit from services on offer
> publicity and the promotion of the IS to the organization (it is this opportunity and its potential which we shall be examining in detail elsewhere in this book).

All the above will need to be written up, and costings and a timescale calculated as to when the work is to be carried out. We elaborate on these actions in Chapter 2.

Scope

When you are producing your service plan, you will need to think in the widest mode, taking on board all the requirements of the organization, the users, the capabilities of the staff and most of all the priorities which will be demanded.

All this will need to be carefully planned, and you may need to think about having service level agreements for different parts of the organization. More on this in Chapter 5, and we also refer you to our book *The complete guide to preparing and implementing service level agreements* (see Appendix A).

Keeping one step ahead of the customers is essential if the information and library service is to have any success. Each staff member of the information service must keep up to date in a number of areas, and be aware of:

> ➢ what is happening in your own organization, be it a local authority, a company, a government department, an academic institution or a commercial organization
> ➢ what is happening in the information supply industry – especially developments in tools and technology
> ➢ the latest publications in the subject areas covered such as books, reports, standard specifications (national and international), pieces of legislation (European and UK), journals and newsletters
> ➢ the latest electronic publications such as databases, CD-ROMs and Internet-based resources
> ➢ the various strategies – local, national and perhaps international – which may affect your service, eg what the British Library is planning.

Information audits can help

We have shown in our book *Becoming a successful intrapreneur* (see Appendix A) that carrying out an information audit, and knowing what the customer requirements are, really does help you as an information specialist to provide up-to-date information. We know that most customers have expectations, make demands upon the information services (which sometimes cannot be fulfilled), and have perceptions of what the service may or may not provide. This is why we strongly stress the importance of developing a service level agreement, which can be invaluable in helping to deliver the services which you can reasonably be expected to give, and which the customer can reasonably expect to receive. In addition, we show how the customer also has a responsibility to update the IS on future information needs. All these activities, including regular feedback, help shape the delivery of the service plan and help to produce excellent information services.

In the information audit (see also Chapter 3) you will have amassed a great deal of knowledge about your customer base, and you should have a reasonable idea of where your customers are located, the type of information they need (or think they need), their current information demands and most importantly *their* future plans of work. From this knowledge you will be able to help them keep ahead, whether they be lecturers needing to know the latest information so they can keep ahead of their students, or members of the research team in an organization.

With the benefit of the above research and negotiation, you have the key to a super-efficient service – the ability to arrange access to the necessary information before the customers ask for it!

The pluses and minuses of having a service plan

The pluses of having a service plan

> The organization will know what the IS is doing and plans to achieve in the forthcoming year or so.
> Your customers will be able to point to various services and recognize the cost-effectiveness of these services to their work.
> You will have convinced management that the budget you need to be able to deliver the services will be fully utilized.
> You and your colleagues will know the training needs of both staff and users, and can plan the programmes accordingly.
> You, your colleagues and users should be expecting new equipment, which will have been specified. This will keep people interested in the service plan.
> The publicity programme will be kept to schedule, and as each milestone is reached some positive publicity will be published.
> Staff and users will know when exactly their training will be taking place.

> There will be a balanced approach to evaluating the new and emerging technologies and where they fit into the IS developments.

The minuses of having a service plan

> You are committed on paper for all the world to see!
> You need to be fully aware that all users are *not* the friendly people they seem to be, especially if services which they expect do not materialize!

The minuses of not having a service plan

> If you do not have a structured plan, then things tend to slip and you will have even more explaining to do.
> You and your colleagues may be left behind in this fast-moving information industry if training, and where necessary re-training, is not carried out on a systematic basis.
> Without a service plan, you will find that timescales slip, and more explanations will be necessary as to why the IS is not delivering the services.
> Without a service plan it is difficult to have a continuous structured publicity programme.
> Staff and users will perhaps become disenchanted with little action from the IS.
> There will be little advancement because no thoughts have been given to the future development of services, staff and users.

The use of a service plan to change attitudes and perceptions

So why does the IS need to change the attitudes and perceptions of the organization, its staff, the users and others?

To answer that, consider where the information service would be if it did not communicate at all with the organization and the users. We suggest that it would be non-existent in a very short space of time – brutal but true! We could give many examples of where an information service has gone out of business because no one knew it was there or what it did.

5

The senior management wrongly assumed, because they did not use it and knew little of its activities, that it was dispensable.

In worst-case scenarios, the information service did not even do anything to contribute to the core business of the organization, be it a school, an information resource centre, a special or workplace information service, or even an academic information service. So *just having* a service plan will force the information service to communicate with other parts of the organization, the users, the potential users – ie the wider audience, whether inside or outside the organization!

Bridge-building in an organization

During the various negotiations, it is necessary to find out what the users really want the IS to be doing, and to establish it as central to the organization. Often during this type of discussion you will find that it is the IS which acts as the bridge from one group of users to another. We have found in our experiences that in a large organization the IS is the focal point and can have an 'umbrella view' of the whole organization.

Just by suggesting a meeting with a group of users to discuss their future information needs, and possible training requirements, you will remove at a stroke the perception of the IS as a place to which people simply escape, perhaps just to read a newspaper.

From this chapter you will now:

➤ know the definition of a service plan
➤ be able to name some of the pluses and minuses of having a service plan
➤ be able to convince others that your information service is really businesslike in its operation.

Chapter 2
The contents of a service plan

In this chapter we look at important headings to be included within the service plan for your information service (IS):

➤ **services**
➤ **publications acquisitions**
➤ **equipment and materials**
➤ **costing**
➤ **publicity and marketing**
➤ **timescales**
➤ **competitors**.

We also look at collection development policies, consider some of the criticisms that have been levelled at information service plans, and look at why plans fail. (We look at personal plans in Chapter 4.)

The service plan for your library and information service must be a comprehensive document, although as we shall see later, it also needs to be flexible to allow for developments during the course of the plan. In order to make sure that it is comprehensive, you will need to include certain standard headings, to cover the elements that should be present in any kind of IS.

You can look at these services in a number of ways. You will certainly have to manage, and to have plans available for, a number of areas of work where the IS has discretion to act, and where you have control. An example might be acquisitions – whether you buy or borrow your stock, or even search for it online. These are areas where your plan will be the primary document describing your organization's management strategy.

In other areas – for example, accommodation or financial systems – you are unlikely to have total discretion and you will have to fit in with the plans of others. But make sure that those in charge of these other areas of work understand your needs and requirements.

Let us look at those areas of work where the information service will be setting the organization's policy. What should appear in your business service plan?

Services

It is not so obvious any more what libraries and information services do. Of course, the users can read and (usually) borrow books, but what about periodicals? And what about electronic services and the Internet? Does your information service provide tuition and coaching, or put on training events to show users how various services can be used? Do you produce an information bulletin, or publish recommended reading lists over the intranet? Do you manage the organization's web site?

As we show in *The complete guide to preparing and implementing service level agreements* (see Appendix A), you need to spell out even the things that apparently are obvious when providing your service. That book shows how to draw up agreements with other parts of your organization to provide them with an information service. However, even before you do that, you need to make lists of your services and define what each of those services comprises. Without a comprehensive list of services, you will be unable to show your financial managers what you are providing for their money, and you will be in a poor position to argue for funding.

Your plan should therefore include a statement of your services in an early chapter or section. You are probably afraid of stating the obvious in this list, but to people who do not make use of all your services, and are not directly involved in managing them, these definitions are not at all obvious. One very senior public sector manager, for example, could not grasp the distinction between periodicals purchased for retention in the various departments of an agency and those that were circulated and then returned to the information service for storage. It can be quite a complex task to set out these statements, but at the end of the process you will have a set of definitions that will be valuable for a range of uses.

Remember that you may need to include a glossary, too, because other managers may see North American and other literature that uses different terminology (eg 'journal routing' for periodical circulation, 'jobber' for agent, and so on).

Try to show what benefits or outcomes the service provides to your clients – for instance, in many organizations people seem to think that newspapers are delivered to the office by some kind of local paper boy rather than as a result of the work of the library and information service.

Set out your standards wherever possible in the course of the definition, as this will provide you with some means of measuring your achievements against your service plan.

For example, here is a possible statement of service for a newspaper cuttings service:

Newspaper cuttings service

The IS will compile a bulletin of cuttings relevant to the Charity and its work from all newspapers available in the information service at 9.00 am each working day, and will distribute it by internal messenger by 10.30 am in 98% of cases. Late editions and evening newspapers will be covered by a further bulletin at 3.00 pm, which will be the latest time for any daily bulletin to appear. On request, the IS will provide guidance on the law of copyright as to which cuttings may be further copied.

Publications acquisitions

Here, too, you need to set out your services, and plans for those services, clearly. It may *seem* obvious that you acquire and process publications but it is not. Whom do you undertake this service for? What are the conditions and target times? And how is repayment organized? A collection development policy (considered later in this chapter) will help you to define some of these points, clarify the options and support the process of estimating the likely financial cost of acquisitions. Your policy can be placed in an annex to your business plan, allowing it to be updated separately as necessary.

Equipment and materials

It is often surprising exactly what materials and equipment an information service consumes during the course of a typical financial year. Of course, much of the expenditure goes on publications purchases – although you may be surprised how much your staff costs amount to when you add in all the overheads that your staff necessarily consume.

Compile a section of your plan that indicates what equipment you already have, and the expected date and cost of replacement. Include details of equipment that you know will be required during the planning period, as well as estimates for consumables. These consumables should include both general expenses such as computer stationery and specialist materials such as library date labels or the cost of producing borrowers' cards.

The list below is by no means exhaustive, but it should prompt you to make a full inventory of the equipment and materials that you need. You could expand it by checking the catalogues of the stationery and computing companies who supply your organization.

> **Computer equipment and consumables**
>> – computers, printers and associated peripherals and cabling
>> – diskettes, back-up and mass storage media (tapes, Zip disks)
>> – program updates
>> – ink, toner
>> – computer projection equipment and spares.

> **Stationery**
>> – paper, labels
>> – pens, pencils, markers, paperclips, staples
>> – overhead projection materials
>> – library-specific stationery (eg date labels) (likely to be proportionately more expensive than standard stationery)
>> – sticky notes and other essentials.

> **Telephones**
>> – call charges
>> – line rental
>> – fax consumables.

> ➤ **Cameras** and other equipment used to produce borrower cards and security passes.
> ➤ **Maintenance contracts** – likely to be 15% of the original equipment price each year. This is a substantial sum and means that you will need to allow roughly twice the purchase price of an item over a five-year costing, even if your calculations allow for the costs of inflation.

All of these and more costs are incurred before you purchase a single publication.

Costing

All of this planning is wasted if it does not include some indication of the likely cost of the service, and how the costs are going to be managed. We saw above that hidden costs like maintenance can add a large amount to the overall price of running an IS, so well-planned financial management is called for.

A sound service plan needs to include the most accurate predictions you can provide of your expenditure on materials and staff in the financial year or other period under consideration. This will include details not only of how much you intend to spend but also when and how you intend to spend it.

Chapter 6 provides some examples of simple financial forecasts and monitoring. These can be adapted to your own situation, and may need amendment to suit your own organization's financial regime.

Publicity and marketing

The service plan must include some indication of how the library and information service will make itself and its services known to users and potential users. A detailed publicity plan should be prepared, although it is probably best published as a separate document from the main plan, or at least incorporated into an annex to your planning document. Keith Hart's book *Putting Marketing Ideas into Action* (see Appendix A) provides an introduction to techniques that will enable you to develop a marketing plan. Using this plan, you can set out the route by which the library and information service will move from its present position to the point where its target market is well informed and makes best use of the services on offer.

Timescales

Most service plans will be designed to fit the funding institution or service's financial year, and financial forecasts and other details will be charted against that year. The calendar timing varies: most organizations follow the tax year and plan from April in one year to March in the following year, but others follow the fiscal years of other countries or are non-standard for other reasons.

This has an incidental effect on your ability to carry out projects to time at certain times of the year, or to obtain supplies quickly. Because many organizations follow the April-to-March financial year, and are unable to carry unspent funds from one year to the next, they occupy the period from January to March attempting to spend money before it literally vanishes from their budgets. This in turn means that suppliers and consultants are very busy during this period, helping to get as much done as possible in the available time. The consequence for those on different planning timescales is that for this period of the year it can be more difficult to obtain consultants to work on projects or to get some materials delivered quickly.

More generally, you should plan to complete projects where possible well before the end of your financial accounting period. You will need to use a project planning tool in order to predict the elapsed time for your project, and to ensure that your start date gives you sufficient time to finish the work before the end of the period. Software tools such as Microsoft Project will give you the means of managing projects on your desktop computer, whilst formal project management methods such as PRINCE (see Appendices A and C) will give you an effective method of ensuring that your projects are well controlled. Build some leeway into your plans for staff who go sick, or for consultants who are unavailable. Always allow some additional time for surprises.

Competitors

You may reckon that yours is an area of information work where there is no competition and so this element can be excluded from your business planning process. In reality almost every IS has some form of competition, and that competition is expanding. It includes bookshops, where people can purchase the books that they think will answer their information requirements, and it certainly includes the Internet, where many people believe the entire stock of the world's wisdom is stored – if only they can find it. If you work in a special information service then you may well see the local public library service as a competitor.

Even if you work in an area where at first analysis there is only apparent collaboration – prison libraries might be one example – there is always an alternative for the users, which is to be non-users. The competition may prove to be the television, or in the example of the prison library, even a collection of books and old periodicals kept on one of the prison wings and which the prison library does not manage.

Your plan needs to address problems of competition. It needs to identify as many as possible of the disincentives and barriers to use, and to set out a strategy for overcoming these blocks. Some of the remedies may be fairly obvious, and some of the tools we discuss in this book (such as a marketing plan) will prove invaluable in tackling these problems. Make a list of the problems and the ways in which you can tackle them. Reckon up the extent of resources, whether financial or in terms of people, that you will have to employ. Highlight any shortage of funds or materials that could prevent you from achieving your target.

Collection development policies

Earlier in this chapter we referred to the establishment of collection development policies as part of your planning process.

What is a collection development policy? There is considerable scope in what to include under this heading. In general it could be defined as a statement of the principal and secondary subject areas that an information service collection will cover, together with an indication of their importance to the collection and the depth to which the collection will purchase available materials.

In an academic or public library, a collection development policy is likely to indicate that most subjects are to be included in the primary list. In a specialist information service, the subjects in which the organization specializes are the candidates for this main list of topics covered. There will be a range of secondary subjects, which may, for instance, cover the law relating to the organization, or topics relevant to the way it does business, such as communications – and librarianship.

You will find that your subject classification scheme makes a good starting point for a statement of your subject specialisms. You can drill down to a suitable level of detail – perhaps main classes in Dewey or UDC, and up to three decimal places of subdivision where appropriate. The hierarchical arrangement of most widely used subject classification schemes makes it possible to specify different levels within each class if that is appropriate. For some materials (such as the musical scores instanced below) you may find it easier to make specific exceptions from a general or blanket statement of inclusion.

It is important next to rank the topics to indicate the depth of collection and thus to show readers which are the spending priorities. The depth of collection might, for example, include:

➢ all relevant material published in English in the UK, Ireland or North America
➢ all relevant material published in Europe
➢ all commercially published material from the UK (ie excluding report and grey literature)
➢ all items appearing in the British National Bibliography and classified in Dewey class 388.3 and its subdivisions
➢ all UK-published children's books costing under £15.00 apiece, excluding board books
➢ all newly published miniature scores of works by composers M–N except Mozart
➢ periodicals, reports and online services only.

Each of these depths has implications for the financial and stock management of the collection, and for related issues such as accommodation.

You can see the impact that delivery times will have on your service, and the effect that a decision to collect grey literature will have in terms of time taken dealing with small publishers, or waiting for them to send the items you have ordered. You can understand that the decision to purchase material from outside the UK will have an impact on your financial accounting systems, as they will have to deal with variable exchange rates against the dollar and the euro. If you decide to focus on electronic services rather than on printed materials, then you will need to forecast your costs differently, and without the aid of so many external sources of help (such as published tables of periodical price movements).

A separate part of your collection development policy should be your retirement policy for the information materials – which is just as important as your policy for adding items to the collection.

Is yours a steady-state library or information service? In that case, you may need to retire materials after a certain length of time – for periodicals, a stated number of years; for books, five years or the publication of a new edition (whichever comes sooner). Alternatively, you might allocate fixed shelf space to each particular subject and weed that section to fit. Whichever way you do it, you need to set the policy down.

Or are you in the lucky position of being able to expand your information service into further space? In that case, you can state that you will continue to collect all material within the scope of your policy, in the knowledge that you will be able to house it. However, do not overlook the costs that come with this freedom, for, as we shall see, if you intend to acquire new shelving or even to clean what you already have, you will need to forecast the cost and account for it.

Your service plan should ideally include some kind of contingency policy. In some organizations, money can vanish during the course of a year as unexpected financial crises strike in other areas of the organization. When this happens, the information service is (wrongly) thought of as an easy option for a 'dawn raid', with the result that what looked like an ample budget is suddenly pared. As the journals renewal bill turns up in many organizations at the very point in the financial year when the appalling truth becomes clear about likely overspending, it helps greatly if the IS possesses an agreed statement of its spending policies. It may even be possible to show what would happen if the organization decided to impose cuts on periodical renewals as a means of bailing out its bad managers in other departments. Nevertheless, it helps to know which subscriptions or titles you would defend to the last, and which could be sacrificed to stave off total closure. Needless to say, careful planning and financial management will always ensure that it is not the IS which provokes such a crisis!

Problems with information service plans

The consideration of an annual information service plan is a vast subject and a detailed analysis is outside the scope of this volume. But some of the criticisms made of existing service plans can offer some pointers to best practice in the whole range of information service planning.

First, many plans are much too long. Be succinct. Structure your plan with plenty of headings and a good index. Say what you intend to achieve, indicate broadly how you intend to achieve it, and how you will know when you have achieved it. If you must explain in detail, leave this to another document or an annex. Say how much your plans will cost, and when you will spend the money.

Resist the temptation to use any documentation that happens to be around in order to pad out the plan. People do not have time to read long plans. Even if you put these other reports into appendices, they still deter the reader by making the plan look unreadable (which it may well be).

The target audience

A single plan cannot as a rule successfully address several audiences. You may need to create separate documents, or to target different parts of a single document at separate audiences, in order to inform such varied groups as your local managers, your users, the Department of Culture, Media and Sport, the University Grants Committee, the Treasury, or whoever needs a high-level plan for their own planning purposes. This is another reason why you should not use documents from other submissions in your plan unless you are sure they are appropriate. What works for your Leisure Services Committee will not be very helpful for most public library users. They may dislike being given formal committee submissions instead of customer-focused information, whilst the money men may just think you are trying to obscure something.

Service plans need to be suitable for use as a management tool. They are not a chore to be written to satisfy budget committees and external scrutineers.

Why plans fail

IS plans can fail for a number of reasons. These reasons can apply equally well to a single project plan as to a regional plan or even a personal plan.

Lack of realism

There is only so much that can be done with the available resources. Unless you are certain that you can get sufficient staff and money (try asking three months before the end of the financial year) do not promise the earth, or promise to do too much too soon. A sensible plan of action will help. Lack of resources, and the inevitable failure to deliver on promises, will lead to disillusion and cynicism.

Lack of flexibility

Things change, and plans should change accordingly. They should be living documents, and as Chapter 6 suggests, they should be continuously updated in the light of developments and progress.

Lack of faith

Planning should not be seen solely as a paper exercise. You can make things happen and deliver improvements, but you need to be sensible. Plan to suit yourself, not others. Negotiate a timescale that allows both parties to be confident of the outcome.

Lack of precision

Many plans fail to say what they are actually about. In such cases it is difficult to tell whether they have been successful, as it is not clear what should even be regarded as success. Set out the stall carefully, and ask someone else to do a reality check to ensure that another reader can understand what you are proposing and when you propose to deliver it. If there is no discernible output or benefit, you need to do more work on the plan.

However, just because a plan is weak, it does not mean that the service that it relates to is poor.

In this chapter we have considered:

➤ several examples of the kinds of headings that you should consider for your service plan
➤ target audiences that your plan should address
➤ how a collection development policy can make your task easier
➤ some of the common problems that have been identified in service plans.

Chapter 3
Why go it alone?
Involving others in your service plan

In this chapter we consider:

➤ why an information audit is essential before you compile a service plan
➤ who else should be involved in developing your service plan
➤ what kind of buy-in you should aim to get from others
➤ how to record your plan
➤ how to register the commitments from others.

No man or woman (or information and library service) is an island. Certainly you are at liberty to draw up plans of work for all kinds of activities as well as your overall information service plan. But your work is wasted if you fail to take account of what others are doing around you and hence fail to deliver the services that you plan. You need not only to take account of others, but to ensure that they buy in to your plans in some way – either by supporting you, or at least by not doing anything that prevents you from achieving your plan.

Information audit

In *Becoming a successful intrapreneur* (see Appendix A) we advocate looking at the aims and objectives of the organization and their relevance to the information professional. We advise that the information professional who has an understanding and appreciation of these issues is far better able to provide a service that appears relevant in the eyes of the senior managers and other influential figures in the organization. Operating a service that appears to be in a vacuum, or somehow isolated from the needs of the organization, brings the danger of the service being sidelined or even closed, when with a better understanding of the issues the information service could fulfil an essential role.

Information professionals face one of their most difficult jobs in getting a clear understanding of their organization so as to be able to provide an information service that is central to the organization. The other side of this coin is that they also have to get the organization to understand the nature of professional information management, particularly in sectors such as finance, management and government, where every member of staff could be said to be an information worker.

A key element is for information professionals to do this in a way that emphasizes their understanding of the organization, rather than appearing to mount a defence of an information service under attack, or even set up some form of counter-culture.

Organizations generally have a wealth of information that is held by the various departments, divisions, sections and even individual staff members. Before a relevant service can be provided, the information professional needs to build up a picture of the organization's information assets, their relationship to one another, and the areas in which they are deficient (causing people to go elsewhere for information or use informal networks).

The tool by which this is done is an information audit – a method that has just as much potential in public service and academic environments as in the special information services where it was first developed. It is an important and valuable technique that yields data about the information resources held within the organization or community, its match to the information requirements of the customer group, and the opportunities for intrapreneurial behaviour.

An information audit will seek to answer a number of questions about information and its use in the organization. It will pose a number of questions that should persuade management (or the people funding the service) of the value of time and effort spent on the information audit activity. And it will consider a number of problems that may be met in the organization's use of information. Further information can be found in *Becoming a successful intrapreneur* and in other texts given in Appendix A.

Who should be involved in your service plan?

A number of people have a vested interest in your service plan. These include:

> ➢ for your organizational service plan: staff, colleagues, customers and suppliers
> ➢ for your personal plan: staff, colleagues and maybe peers in other organizations.

Staff and colleagues

People who work with and for you must be taken into account when you establish your service plan, whether it is for the organization and the IS that you are responsible, or your own personal and professional development.

Unless you are a one-person band, you will need to think about what your staff can deliver and when they will be able to deliver. It is no use including major tasks in your plan that need to be carried out in August if your deputy takes leave in that month because of school holiday dates. You cannot expect a small team to deliver several projects simultaneously when it needs to provide induction tours for new students, or for new council members following scheduled elections.

Whatever kind of organization or community you work in, you need to consult your colleagues in other departments before assuming that you can depend on their being able to deliver a service or a product that you need.

The kind of service or product may be quite varied, both in its complexity or nature, and in the way it is delivered. It may be, for example, that you need a professional service such as your legal department to help you to complete a tender document. If you schedule this without consultation, you might find the legal department is committed to dealing with a pending court case or advising on a major review at the time when you had planned to have their opinion. You may plan to launch a new press cuttings service to provide a bulletin to the management floor at 10.00 am, but without the cooperation of the messenger service your newspapers may not reach you until then! Check that they can cope with

21

the schedules you need before adding this new service to your plan. Check that you will not need to make additional and unplanned payments to get the service you require.

You probably need to consult extensively with some colleagues. Your organization's training service may either supply you directly with courses, or perhaps pass on the more specialized requirements to external training organizations such as The Library Association. You in turn may well offer information support to trainees, and supply reading lists, special selections of supporting publications or some other service. You may provide standalone computers for self-guided studies. In cases like this, quite extensive liaison is needed. You should ideally know the training service's plans for the next year, in order to know not only what items you need to have available for trainees, but also when there is likely to be some slack time to schedule training for the information staff. You should also know something about the funds that are likely to be available.

Customers

Customers can be a real hindrance at times! Has someone from somewhere in your organization ever told you that a major project needs extra information resources during the two weeks when you had planned a stocktake? Have you ever had to cancel a training course because of an unexpected rush of work that wasn't urgent two weeks before? If it hasn't happened to you, you have probably heard of someone that it did happen to.

Sharing plans with your customers can help to avoid this. If you visit your users on a regular basis, you can take some of the time to tell them of major plans in your schedule, and ask for information about any major projects that they would like the information service to help them with. You may have a number of other channels through which these messages can be exchanged, such as the information services newsletter, a staff newspaper or an intranet. You could even display posters announcing plans for major changes, and see what information and comment these elicit.

Of course there will always be some unexpected crises – that is the way of things. But if you need to go on a training course to use the new software version of your main database host, then it is unfair of a major customer to prevent you through their bad planning. In the end, it is to the detriment of all the customers in your organization. You can make a positive feature of some of these reductions in service by explaining how your plan includes improved services after the various training courses that you and your staff will be undertaking during the course of the year.

It is important to discover whether your customers are planning any major initiatives of their own, especially if you find that two or more major events are likely to happen at the same time and that your information service may be coping with urgent demands from several quarters at once. Enter the information you receive in your time chart, and allow generous margins of error, as people tend not to deliver on the exact day scheduled. (The only exception to this might be in a public organization, at the end of a financial year, because of all the accounting problems that can otherwise follow.) Try to develop the skill of identifying the risks to your plans, and to other people's, so that you can make some reasonably accurate guesses at the real timing of events, and for that matter the real costs of the ones that you are involved with.

Suppliers

Do not forget the role of your suppliers in helping you both to create and to deliver your service plan. Suppliers have the advantage of knowing what is happening in a wide range of types of libraries and information centres. Their own plans for new products or services are often based on the requirements of a number of their customers, and their announcement of a new initiative can provide you with an element of your own plan.

Indeed, the very fact that your supplier has plans for the products and services that you use means that you have to feature these events in your own plan. You may well decide that you do not want to migrate to the new version of your serials software, but it should be a decision that you take positively and record, rather than one which simply happens through your inertia. When will your supplier withdraw the version you now use, or leave it unsupported? Do you need to plan to bring maintenance in-house, or to migrate to the new software before the change happens?

Is it possible to make regular contact with your suppliers to learn their plans? Are there open days and user meetings that you can attend, or can their representative call on you or telephone you at regular intervals? All of these events should feature on your service plan, and you should ensure that any decisions regarding the suppliers' services and products will fall due after rather than before these contacts. You might just discover that all your plans are based on the availability of a product that is about to go off the market.

You may need to convince your colleagues that consulting your suppliers and planning on the basis of their advice is a sensible course of action. They may not be aware that changing suppliers is a long and sometimes painful business, so that it is easier to postpone the development of a service for a few months until your supplier can offer it, rather than going to a different supplier who does. (Again, this does not preclude you from making sensible checks such as a value-for-money audit of serials prices – but make sure that this event appears in your service plan. In that way you can point to the forthcoming check as evidence that you are managing the supplier and not the other way around.)

Persuading others to cooperate

You may well have to work hard to get others to buy in to your plans. But it is nevertheless important to do so, and to make sure that your colleagues and suppliers are aware of your plans. In some organizations, business planning is an important element of the way that they work. In others, planning is slack or non-existent.

Libraries and information centres could argue that their business is demand-led, so that they do not know what is going to happen later in a business year. This much is probably true, but it does not follow that you should not plan for what *can* be predicted, nor does it follow that you cannot plan in order to have some control over these events.

The lesson really comes down to this: marketing, marketing and marketing. If you take your plan out to the customers, discuss it with your suppliers, and involve your staff in the planning process, then it can be an active tool for developing the information service. It can be a method that ensures there is time for staff training and development, and for adequate rest – no more abandoned holiday plans! When you have talked through and agreed a plan with all the other players, you can feel satisfied that you have done your best by them, and it is reasonable for you to be able to expect them to support your plans too.

Setting down your plan

In all of these cases you need to check what other commitments exist and to look at other people's plans before deciding your own. Setting out the plan against some of the existing information (like holiday charts) will be a valuable starting point. How best can you do this?

A number of aids are available that will help. Many people have a personal organizer, which is no longer the exclusive prerogative of city financial dealers and the like. A wide range of paper refills is available, including the year-at-a-glance annual planning charts that are invaluable for spotting timing conflicts and problems. Any kind of chart that allows you to see a long period of time at once – maybe a month or more – will be useful, whilst some of the larger-sized inserts permit quite sophisticated planning, allowing you to plot details such as the availability of particular people or resources.

More specialized still are the glossy calendar inserts that come with coloured sticky strips to allow you to plot periods of time, and assorted stars and dots to place particular events. These are, of course, miniature versions of the wall charts that come with similar stick-on accessories. Or you could just take some squared paper and make your own.

Work-planning software for computers is more sophisticated, and allows you to visualize your plans in order to see the dependencies on other sections or people. It also helps you to see the minimum time that a project can take, and to be sure that you have not set impossible deadlines. Suppose, for example, that the head of cataloguing cannot receive training in your new software package until the end of May. You need to ensure, therefore, that tasks demanding specialist knowledge of this software are not allocated until June. By showing this training or knowledge as a resource that is not available until that date, you can ensure that peo-

25

ple do not waste their time waiting for this knowledge to be available before progressing with the service plan. The software usually allows you to see several views of the work plan, so that you could look at the times when staff are required for a project, or at the timing of the stages of the plan.

Recording other people's commitments

As part of these activities, it is useful to make a record of the commitments and other information that you receive from your colleagues and suppliers. At one level, recording training plans is an important activity that should form part of every manager's work. Indeed, if your organization holds, or plans to hold, an accreditation such as Investors in People, or is applying techniques such as the Business Excellence Model, practices such as this will form part of the activities that you will be called on to perform. At the other extreme, a record of commitments will prove useful when, as often happens, one is left in the position of having to explain 'what went wrong'. We hope yours is an organization that does not use blame as a weapon (though if it is, you can be ready with an answer). Rather, use your record as a learning and planning tool, so that your estimates of events and their timing will be more accurate next time.

Show other people's contributions on your plans, and if it is appropriate to share the plan with other sections, send them a copy, making sure that they see where their commitment lies. Write and share commentaries, or send out the minutes of information services planning meetings where the contributions of your colleagues are recorded. Show colleagues where their section appears as a resource in your plans and where you plan to provide a service to their projects. Ask whether these represent a correct version of their own plans, and obtain their positive assent. Check from time to time if you do not hear from them, and make sure you discuss progress with them on their visits to the information centre. Learn to gather information by informal as well as formal means.

By keeping your records up to date, you will be able to see where priorities have changed or appear to have done so. Call up your colleagues and ask what has happened to their planned products, or services, or projects. You may remind them that the library and information centre could play a part in helping them out. You will be able to see whether a change in their plans is likely to increase or decrease pressure later in the year, allowing you to make the case for extra staff, some training, or even a well-earned holiday.

In this chapter we have seen:

➤ why an information audit is essential
➤ how colleagues and staff all have a contribution to make to the service plan
➤ why suppliers are important to your service plan
➤ some of the ways to persuade people to commit to your service plans and to support you
➤ some of the ways that can be used to record your service plan.

Chapter 4
Your personal plan
Personal and professional development plans

In this chapter we look at:

➢ why you need a personal and professional development plan
➢ how to identify your development needs
➢ how to plan the additional development you need
➢ which sources of information and help you can use to guide you
➢ how personal plans fit into the service plan for your LIS and your organization.

Alongside your service plan for your organization, you should consider creating a personal and professional development plan for yourself and for any colleagues that you manage. You could also offer advice on creating such a plan to anyone whom you mentor or advise on career matters.

Where do you want to be in three, five or ten years' time? In our book *Your successful LIS career* (see Appendix A), we advised you to consider this question in order to start preparing the way. We suggested that the answer would be different depending on your age and the stage that your career had reached, but that your ideas should be taking shape. In particular you should be thinking about what you need to do, and what new skills you will need, to get where you want to be. Whilst you cannot predict everything that is likely to happen in ten years' time, you can make some reasonable guesses about three and five years. You probably have a good idea already about some of the professional skills you need to develop, and know enough about the state of technologies under development to predict the level of technical expertise that you will need.

Without some idea of the actions that you will take to achieve whatever personal development you want, you are unlikely to succeed. The way that you lay out a systematic campaign to reach your goal is with a personal and professional development plan. You should be able to inter-mix personal and professional goals in a plan. Sometimes one goal will serve both purposes. You may, for example, decide to achieve a particular qualification, or to obtain a secondment to another part of the organization to gain wider experience. These actions will not only benefit you but also your employer's business – or your own – by making the services that you offer more attractive.

Compiling your plan – documentation

How can documentation be used in creating your personal plan of action? It can be useful in a number of ways:

> ➢ It can enable you to define where you are now.
> ➢ It can enable you to define the steps you should take to achieve your target.
> ➢ It can enable you to decide when to take those steps and how much to invest in each step in terms of time or money (whether your own money or your employer's training budget).
> ➢ It can enable you to record your progress along that path, and to celebrate your eventual arrival at that goal.

This is really not much different from what can be seen happening in other areas of work, where we were talking about investment in information services. You will use the same sort of approach as in devising a project plan or an annual service plan for the information service, only for you as a person.

Question: 'How do you eat an elephant?' Answer: 'One piece at a time!' Look at the logical steps along the way, and decide when and how you can invest in them. Then set out your plan, and monitor your progress against it. You will find this is invaluable if you have any kind of annual review of work, as you can use the document to chart your professional progress. You can even use this approach in your personal life – whether your personal goal is to lose ten pounds in weight, to complete next year's London Marathon, or to amass enough money to retire five years early – the same techniques of planning and monitoring will carry you through.

There are a number of documents available to help you create a personal development plan for your work in libraries and information centres. They take one of two broad approaches:

> ➢ The first approach is to provide a **framework document** that gives you a structure within which you can identify the skills that you need to acquire in order to reach a higher level along your path. These will vary depending on the ambitions that you want to satisfy and will be individual and personal to you, as will the plan that you devise for reaching your particular goal. This kind of planning is based on a workbook that you complete as you progress. You can amend the goal because you have set it yourself, and you can adjust your requirements and the programme of work in the light of any changes and developments.
> ➢ The other approach is to identify the skills that are needed for particular tasks or types of task, and to publish a document that lists those **skills and competencies** that anyone who aspires to similar jobs should possess. In that way you can identify the training and development that you need to schedule before you apply for this level and type of job.

But, if you use the framework approach, how do you identify the skills to put into your plan? After all, there is a lot of blank space to fill. In fact, combining the two approaches gives you an excellent way to plan your personal development.

Guidance and frameworks

If you are a member of The Library Association, you will have a copy of the *Framework for Continuing Professional Development* (CPD) for your personal use (see Appendix A). A few other professional bodies for librarians have similar documents. One example is the Australian Library and Information Association's career development kit (see

Appendix A). If you and/or your employer are members of the Institute of Personnel and Development, you could look at the CPD material which they issue.

If you prefer to start with the list of skills and competencies, you have a wide choice of documents that are available to help you. These fall into two further groups:

> The first group gives you a list of the competencies you need in information science and librarianship expressed in general categories. You can find a British list in the Institute of Information Scientists' *Criteria for Information Science,* or an American-based one in the Special Libraries Association's *Competencies for Special Librarians of the 21st Century* (see Appendix A). These lists identify the skills that are associated with library and information work, but do not of course indicate the balance of skills that you need to be a candidate for your target job.

> The second group of documents works by listing a range of posts, and partly or fully identifying the particular skill and experience requirements for each. If you read French, a good example of this approach is taken by the ADBS (see Appendix A), which lists a number of different job types (*métier-types*), which it then analyses in terms of the skills and experience that are needed. In some sectors of librarianship, work has been done on specialist competencies. For example, Government librarians in the UK have access to a list of competencies designed for them by a subcommittee of the Committee of Departmental Librarians, showing the skills that are required at each of the four grade levels in Civil Service libraries. (At present this work is not published. A revision is currently proposed to include new areas of library work such as those based around the Internet.) With this information you can plan to acquire the training and on-the-job knowledge that are needed to take on this type of work.

Use these lists to help you to identify those skills that you need to acquire through training and those that you need to obtain through work experience, perhaps by doing another job on a posting or secondment. Arrive at a realistic estimate of when you could expect to take on a job of the kind you want, and slot in the training courses you need. Use the various catalogues issued by the professional bodies to identify the courses you need, and then add these to the timetable in your plan. Transfer these details to your workbook, but maintain a future timetable of courses and other activities that you will need to schedule into your normal working life.

Your training plan might schedule the following activities :

> Identify your goal (particular job, new qualification, etc) and any constraints.
> Identify and list the skills you need in order to achieve your goal and overcome the constraints.
> Determine the level of skill you wish or need to acquire.
> Identify any additional experience that you need to obtain.
> Decide whether obtaining these skills and experience is a short-, medium- or long-term objective.
> Identify the types of CPD activity that will help you to acquire these skills or experience.
> Identify the places where you can gain the experience you need.
> Decide which activities you can take responsibility for outside work, and which ones can only be done with the help and/or cooperation of your employer.
> Take time to plan, record and review these activities.

The last point is an important one. Work planning, whether for CPD or for any other part of the business of the library and information service, takes time. It needs a clear space in your schedule, not a series of five-minute breaks grabbed in between meetings, or a time when you are constantly interrupted. Personal planning can be usefully carried out with a mentor or other trusted colleagues; and plans of work in general work far better when you have the involvement and agreement of everyone affected. Even if there is insufficient time to consult on the first draft and you have to sketch it out alone, be sure to consult others as far as possible before you submit the final version to your management. Even if nothing is changed as a result of the consultation, your colleagues will feel much more strongly that they own part of the plan and are committed to its success.

Planning CPD for your organization

This planning activity is even more important if you are responsible for the management of training and professional development in the organization where you work. You will need to juggle the requirements for several people and match them against the available training courses and other facilities such as computer-based training materials. There will be financial matters to resolve as well, since much of the training will have to be paid for from your budgets. The detail is beyond the scope of this book but you can find more information in the further reading given in Appendix A.

Expecting the unexpected

You can plan ahead to a considerable extent but it is difficult to foresee every eventuality. In terms of career plans and personnel management, you cannot tell, for example, when a job that features in your plan will suddenly become available because the job holder is moving to a post somewhere else. This applies even more if you are planning the training for several people in a section. You cannot predict when you will have an unexpected vacancy to fill, with the consequent need to arrange further training to ensure that someone else is skilled enough to take on the work. This can be difficult at short notice, so a part of your plan might be to ensure that all your staff attend training to allow them to shadow each other's jobs. This would benefit both their own career development and the IS by ensuring skilled back-up in case of unexpected absences.

Although the major providers of training now publish annual catalogues giving the dates for their courses throughout the year, there are many short courses – often provided by special-interest groups and the smaller training groups – which are only announced a few weeks before the date. All you can do in this case is to keep a list of requirements with very broad dates ('summer or autumn 2001?') and wait to see what is offered through the mailshots you receive and the postings to library discussion lists.

Fitting your personal plan into the information service plan

Your personal plan does not of course stand in isolation from that of any colleagues that you may work with, or from the IS itself (even if you are a one-person band). Your training needs and other development activities must be fitted into the overall service plan, whilst the IS service plan needs to take account of the fact that you and your colleagues will be away from the workplace on training courses. This means that both time and money have to be built into the budgets, and that any planned projects have to take account of your planned absences. If you are planning, for example, to open a new Internet authoring service, then you should make sure that the project plan includes technical tasks such as obtaining the hardware and software needed and having telecommunications lines installed. But you also need to ensure that it includes time and funds for training someone to use this new equipment to produce the required outputs and outcomes. Plans must be realistic. If the next suitable course is not being run until the beginning of October, there is no point in planning to open the service in mid-September. You may need to point this out firmly to your own managers, as in their own areas of work they may be used to training being available on demand.

Your personal plan must reflect these training requirements and the costs involved. You can obtain realistic costings from training directories issued by your suppliers, or by ringing them for information, or by looking on their websites. You can estimate the likely cost of courses from smaller suppliers by looking at course announcements on mailing lists. Don't forget to add the cost of travel and meals, and perhaps even the cost of hiring a temporary member of staff if an absence of a week is involved.

Plan from the top down as well as from the bottom up. As well as deciding whether your own development plans require time and perhaps money from the organization, you should be considering how the organization's future development will impact on members of the LIS staff. Will someone need to be trained in Internet technology, or to set part of their training time aside for training on the new library system being installed in the autumn? The final plan should reflect the needs of both staff and employer, and, by giving the staff the training opportunities they require, it should ensure that the information service can move forward with the security that comes with a fully trained and competent staff.

In an organization that compiles and distributes business plans as part of its management style, there will be a cascade that starts with the corporate plan. This will dictate the content of the information service plan, which will be designed to support the corporate plan. In turn, the IS plan will help to highlight the training and other skills acquisition activities that individual members of staff will need to undertake in order to ensure that the IS business plan is successful.

After reading this chapter you should understand:

➢ why personal plans are important for everyone who works in LIS
➢ why those personal plans are an important part of LIS planning
➢ how to go about compiling your personal plan and where to find guidance
➢ how your personal plan is reflected in IS training plans, IS business plans and your corporate business plan.

Chapter 5
Evaluating and monitoring your service plan

> **In this chapter we consider:**
>
> ➤ **how often to monitor your plan**
> ➤ **how to assess the service covered by your plan**
> ➤ **how to cope with customers' requests for services not in your plan**
> ➤ **how to introduce new services to your plan.**

In Chapter 6 we shall be looking at some of the consequences of these issues as we discuss revisions of your plan.

Monitoring the plan

There are a number of ways to monitor your plan. Your organization will probably require you to carry out some of these forms of monitoring and make a regular return, but you might decide to add some of the other forms to give you additional valuable information about your users and the ways in which you are serving them.

Formal reports will probably include financial returns and statistics of performance. Other means of monitoring might include surveys, either by observing and interviewing users or by issuing questionnaires. You will also probably be asked to provide a report on your achievements during the lifetime of your plan. In this you can provide more narrative and explanation about events and progress.

Purchasing budgets and financial monitoring

Information services will have a budget allocation that must be accounted for to the financial authorities in your organization. This may be a finance department or possibly a committee that is responsible for your allocation of funds. It is a useful guiding thought that, whatever the mechanism that provides you with the budget, the money is likely to have come from library users. They may be chargepayers, taxpayers or subscribers to the organization; but whatever they are, the money has been provided voluntarily or through statutory powers assigned to the organization, so you have a responsibility to account for it properly.

Your service plan will certainly include information about the materials and services that you will be buying on behalf of your users. You will need to provide a plan of the way that you will be spending these funds, and you will need to monitor the outgoing expenditure and commitments. With the monitoring information you can decide whether you are still on course, and what action if any you need to take to remain within budget for the reporting period.

Information services budgets generally give financial managers a headache. Finance departments like budgets that are spent in equal portions across a financial year, because there are few surprises. Underspending in one month can generally be seen as a saving, or if not will be corrected by additional expenditure the following month. Information services have some budgets that follow this pattern – staff salaries are one example. The two factors that are most likely to influence the steady level of spending are pay increases and staff changes. A pay increase means that if the likely month of payment and a possible amount are known, then the profile can be easily established (see example in Figure 5.1).

So, although there are some variations through the year, the salary bill for the IS is fairly constant and predictable. In practice there will be further variations. For example, although you have included the expected retirement in your salary predictions, you cannot anticipate resignations that may take place during the year. Consider what might happen in that instance. Suppose that the first four months go according to plan before the senior assistant librarian takes a better job in another IS. This means that the salary bill will now reduce by the amount of her salary until the replacement is in post. The new person may be less experienced so that he gets less salary than his predecessor in the post. In that case we might get a revised salary prediction that looks something like the table in Figure 5.2.

Barsetshire Libraries and Information Services

Central Library staff budget

Assumptions

➢ A 2.5% pay rise will be paid from July, with back pay in November.

➢ When a predicted retirement occurs at the end of October, the member of staff will not be replaced until January.

April	£15,000	The basic pay bill.
May	£15,000	
June	£15,000	
July	£15,000	
August	£15,000	
September	£15,000	
October	£16,500	The 2.5% rise, with £1125 for three months' back pay and £375 for the current month.
November	£14,375	A normal month for the £375 pay rise, but now there is a retirement vacancy too.
December	£14,375	
January	£15,375	The retirement vacancy is filled.
February	£15,375	
March	£15,375	
	£181,375	Total salary bill for the year.

Fig. 5.1 *A sample staff budget constructed on the basis of a planned pay rise*

April	£15,000	The basic pay bill.
May	£15,000	
June	£15,000	
July	£15,000	Senior assistant librarian resigns (salary £1500 pm).
August	£13,500	
September	£13,500	
October	£14,550	The 2.5% rise, with £1050 for three months' back pay – the SAL qualifies for only one month (July) so £75 is deducted.
November	£12,875	A normal month for the £375 pay rise, but now there is a retirement vacancy too.
December	£14,275	A new senior assistant librarian arrives. He earns £100 less than his predecessor.
January	£15,275	The retirement vacancy is filled.
February	£15,275	
March	£15,275	
	£174,525	Total budget for salaries this financial year.

Fig. 5.2 *The sample budget revised as a result of a staff resignation*

This kind of monitoring is relatively straightforward even where unpredictable staff changes take place. You will get some sympathy from other parts of your organization in your management of this part of the budget, because these things happen to every section that employs staff (in other words, everyone). But you will get far less sympathy in the monitoring of services that serve only the IS, because of the way that they function.

Think for a moment about purchasing goods from outside companies for your organization. In general, the things that organizations buy fit into one of a few distinct types:

➢ They may buy lots of identical things that are cheap, like paperclips or pens – and it doesn't really matter if the supplier offers you a different brand when your choice is out of stock.

➢ They may buy a number of identical things that are quite expensive, and with a detailed specification, such as a particular type of computer or printer.

➢ They may buy specified services like consultancy or project management for a particular job or project.

Information services do not fit this pattern. Certainly they may buy paperclips, computers and consultancies, but many purchases don't work in the way they do in the rest of the organization:

➢ They may buy lots of cheap but different things like books, where a different brand is no use if the type you order is out of stock. Even when the price is known, a book may turn up at a completely different price, and it may have a completely different label on it because the title has changed (but not the author).

➢ They may buy a number of identical and quite expensive things with a detailed specification like periodicals, but unlike computers these are delivered in parts over the period of a year, and there is no way of knowing that a part is missing until the one after it turns up instead.

➢ They may buy specified services like online databases, but they don't know how much they need until after they have finished using them, and they don't know which projects are going to use them until they ask.

You can add further problems. Books are exempt from VAT, for example, but some of the items that libraries buy are taxed in part and create odd rates that are rejected by accounting department computers. For example, on a book with an attached CD-ROM, the CD attracts VAT but the book does not; and many corporate subscriptions are partly VAT-exempt to reflect the supply of zero-rated and exempt items such as publications as part of the subscription.

To these problems you need to add the difficulty that many libraries receive their bills in two or three large bundles, with a steady flow of unpredictable bills across the year. Instead of a predictable expenditure each month such as might be allocated to computer maintenance, the IS budgets might look like the example in Figure 5.3.

Central Library materials budget

Assumptions
➢ The library pays for its periodicals in December and receives a supplementary invoice in February. The standing orders are renewed in May.
➢ Online usage is relatively steady but increases during college vacations.

	Materials	Online	
April	£2,700	£750	
May	£16,900	£600	Includes standing order renewals.
June	£2,400	£575	
July	£2,200	£640	
August	£1,800	£1,100	Little new publishing but students use the online service.
September	£3,200	£850	
October	£2,800	£450	
November	£2,400	£500	
December	£25,700	£700	Includes periodicals renewals.
January	£2,600	£650	
February	£4,600	£700	Includes supplementary invoices.
March	£3,700	£650	End-year spend on materials.
	£71,000	£8,165	Total materials budget.

Fig. 5.3 *A sample library materials budget*

It should be apparent from this sample profile that your spending pattern is probably very different from that of many of the other parts of your organization. It will be up to you to justify it – and because you are handling things differently from the majority of your colleagues, you need to show that you are managing this pattern of spending efficiently, and that your perceived awkwardness is justified.

Incidentally, you should hold out against being shoe-horned into a particular spending profile just to suit your accounting department's convenience. Some organizations have so-called standard profiles, such as constant spending, or all expenditure in first and last quarter, or whatever may suit. If you accept a pattern that does not reflect your IS clientele and its suppliers' billing cycles, then you will spend time every month explaining why your profile differs from the norm. This is a waste of everyone's time and can be avoided, if necessary, by means of one big argument at the start of the year in which you explain why library and information service budget profiles are unique.

You will need to monitor actual expenditure against this budget in order to check whether you are going to meet your target. There could be a number of factors affecting the predictions. You might, for example, find that your ordering department was understaffed and could not process the orders in time. Equally there could be variations in exchange rates that affect periodicals price predictions – although the major fluctuations of the late 1980s and early 1990s seem thankfully to be a thing of the past.

You will probably be provided with some sort of financial monitoring information extracted from the central accounting system of your organization. It would repay you to develop a suitable spreadsheet on a library computer into which you could enter financial commitments as you make them. If you have ordered a publication at the first announcement of its appearance, you may not have to produce the money for six months, but you will have effectively committed that money even though it does not show up in the accounts. You thus have less to spend than your accountants may be telling you, and will also need to build this commitment into the figures for the expected month of publication. Remember too that you may not receive the invoice at the time of delivery, and that your accounts section may introduce a further delay from the time they receive the bill for payment. It can therefore be some weeks before an order even for a currently available item is processed and charged to your accounts, and you will need a record for your own purposes in the meantime.

If you know something about spreadsheets, you can develop a fairly sophisticated model that works out the amount remaining of your original budget and reallocates it to the remaining months of the year. You should set your original estimates against these new figures to see whether they are realistic, or whether you should be looking to reallocate some of the funds, or to pass them to other sections of the organization.

In our example shown in Figure 5.3, let us suppose that a number of items had come in at a higher price than expected and that there was a supplementary invoice in June after the May standing order renewals bill (see Figure 5.4).

By this stage the actual expenditure is already £4,800 over budget. This is more than the predicted spend for July and August combined! In

	Estimated expenditure	Actual expenditure
April	£2,700	£2,900
May	£16,900	£18,700
June	£2,400	£5,200
July	£2,200	. . .
August	£1,800	
September	£3,200	
October	£2,800	
November	£2,400	
December	£25,700	
January	£2,600	
February	£4,600	
March	£3,700	
	£71,000	

Fig. 5.4 *A sample materials budget showing actual payments against estimates*

other terms, this is a 38% overspend in the first three months and would lead to an out-turn (a year-end total) of almost £98,000 – £27,000 more than allocated.

You need to take some sort of urgent action to correct this pattern. If prices have risen, you should expect your serials renewal to be more than anticipated and allow a further sum – perhaps £1000 – for price increases. You could then reallocate what is left of your original budget to provide new spending targets for the remaining months, or alternatively be prepared to go and argue with management for more money! You will need to have some contingency plans worked out to decide how to manage within the new budget. If you need to tell department heads that you are cutting back on purchases in their subject areas, action taken at this point of the financial year has more chance of success, and those departments affected may be able to find money to help you.

To return to our example, we might now find that the reallocated sums after the first three months look like those given in Figure 5.5.

This is a realistic approach that recognizes not only the value of serials and journal literature to your organization but also the tough targets that will need to be met in order to supply the necessary materials within budget. There are some quite difficult decisions ahead in terms of book selection and other purchasing, but you at least have a rationale for the choices to be made and an indication of what will happen if you shirk those decisions.

If the problem is underspending, then things are different. In this case you should apply the same procedures to obtain both a predicted out-turn at the current rates of expenditure, and the amount that would need to be spent if your original predictions are to be met. Armed with these figures, you can decide whether to splash out on that new set of encyclopaedias, or else to transfer some of the money to another budget.

Performance measures

In a volume of this size there is insufficient room to include an exhaustive description of the use of performance measures. There are other titles that do so and some are listed in the bibliography in Appendix A. However, some consideration must be given to these measures. Your ser-

	Estimated expenditure	Actual expenditure
April	£2,700	£2,900
May	£16,900	£18,700
June	£2,400	£5,200
July	£2,200	£1,652
August	£1,800	£1,352
September	£3,200	£2,403
October	£2,800	£2,103
November	£2,400	£1,803
December	£25,700	£26,700
January	£2,600	£1,953
February	£4,600	£3,455
March	£3,700	£2,779
	£71,000	£71,000

Fig. 5.5 *A sample materials budget revised on the basis of price rises*

vice plan is of little value if it cannot be monitored and evaluated, and the main way in which this can be done is through performance measures.

Library performance measures have developed greatly in recent years. Less than 20 years ago, much of the collection of statistical data about library use seemed to depend on counting things. Books, libraries, librarians – all were counted, and tables published showing how many of each there were. Although there continues to be some value in these, more worth is obtained from measures that attempt to describe development or change.

It is more useful to know how many books there are per user, or how much was spent per user, than to know how many books a library owns and how much it has spent in total. With information in the form of ratios like these, it becomes possible to see how valuable the library has been within its user community, and to compare it with services provided by other organizations even though these may involve quite different user communities in terms of size or other characteristics.

There have been a number of worthwhile attempts over the last ten years to develop performance indicators for libraries and information services. They offer the service manager the opportunity to base both the service plan and its evaluation on firm criteria. This is because they make it possible to set meaningful and measurable targets into the service plan, and then to assess performance against those targets as the planned work is delivered over the course of the accounting period.

Surveys and questionnaires

A library survey or customer questionnaire will help to draw out information that performance indicators do not provide. Even a simply drawn-up form can tell you about your users' likes and dislikes and their habits, but you will get rather more value from a properly designed form. You may have a member of your staff who can do this because they have experience and perhaps qualifications in statistical work, or you could use one of the specialized texts available to help you.

Remember that your users are often busy people who will not willingly fill out long surveys, so you need to devise a short document that will tell you the essential things you need to know. Use open-ended questions to help you do this. For example, you can avoid asking 'Are you a information services user?' by asking 'How many times in a week do you use the information service?' If you provide an answer corresponding to zero, you can still direct people who choose this option to supplementary questions designed to find out why they do not use your services.

Customer requirements

The kinds of calculations indicated above can help you to decide how to meet new customer requirements, or changes in the existing patterns, such as when a section is closed or moves to another location.

If you have a new subject area to cover, you will need to estimate the cost of supplying and servicing the materials needed and then build this cost into your overall figures. People working in the field can tell you what journals and services they need, and your suppliers can give you estimates of the cost of these items for the remainder of the financial year. These figures will tell you whether you can afford the new costs from the existing budget or whether you need to argue for further funding.

But how do you know that you are meeting customers' requirements? And how can you ensure that your plan represents their needs? There are a number of methods that you can use. You may decide that the best idea is to combine several of these:

> Draw conclusions from the performance indicators collected by your library.
> Draw conclusions from the information produced by your automated system.
> Carry out user surveys, either through personal interviews or by means of questionnaires.

You can use these methods to discover users' forthcoming requirements. What new programmes of work are due to begin? What information needs are there? How are these to be reflected in your service plan?

You will also discover whether any of your existing services are no longer in tune with requirements. Perhaps the areas they cover are no longer as important as they once were, or perhaps the decision has been taken to close down an area of research.

All these factors need to be included in revisions of your current plan, which we shall look at in more detail in Chapter 6. A suitable interval for these reviews would be around once a quarter, which allows sufficient time for developments to take place and to have an effect on your service, but still allows time for corrective action if things start to go wrong or there are cuts in budget.

New services

The introduction of new services can be considered in the light of the results of the two processes described above. The results of your surveys and questionnaires may draw your attention to an area of work that is not being properly covered or to a new initiative that is being developed and needs information service support.

The financial monitoring you carry out will allow you to see whether you are likely to have sufficient funds to support the roll-out of the new initiative or service. If you have spare money, the answer is simple: you transfer the spare money to the new service. If you are short of the necessary funds, however, you can predict the effect on your main services by pretending that the start-up costs are in fact an overspend on your present budget. Use the spreadsheet method shown above to incorporate these costs and calculate how funding the new service would impact on your main service. This will show whether it is possible to meet the cost of the new service without further funding; and if further funding is needed, it will indicate the likely amount that you need.

After reading this chapter you will have a good idea about:

➤ **how often to monitor your plan**
➤ **how to assess the service covered by your plan**
➤ **how to cope with customers' requests for services not in your plan**
➤ **how to introduce new services into your plan.**

Chapter 6
'Well, we did a service plan once!'
Ensuring that your service plan stays alive!

In this chapter you will find out:

➢ why continuous assessment of services is necessary for a service plan
➢ how you can use the results from continuous dialogue with customers
➢ why your service plan will need revising when you are introducing new services.

So how often should you revise your service plan?

The simple answer could be 'How long as a piece of string?' Seriously, your service plan needs to be constantly revised. This doesn't mean every day, or even every week, but on a regular basis – perhaps monthly to begin with, then extending the period if the frequency is too high.

In practice it is a bit like carrying out a continuous risk assessment from a health and safety point of view. You need to have your service plan constantly in mind because any alteration you make to any particular area will force you to think about the downstream effect on the other parts of the service plan. For example, if you are introducing a new service which is technology-based, such as the use of the Internet to gain access to journals, you will need think about the following:

➢ Where is the workstation for accessing the service to be located physically?
➢ When will it arrive?
➢ Will staff need training in order to be able to use it effectively?
➢ Will the users need any special training?
➢ What kind of publicity will be needed to inform the users?

> ➢ Will it affect any other service – for example interlibrary loans or document supply?
> ➢ Will other parts of the budget be affected?
> ➢ Will all the services still be on target?

Continuous assessment of services in the service plan

There is a need constantly to assess the effectiveness of any task, service or product. This can be done in a number of ways, but the information staff need to be really honest in the assessment, and to persuade the users to be equally as honest.

So not only does the information manager need to think strategically, but the same applies to all the staff involved in the delivery of the services. Continuous assessment of the service plan checks the timescale and indicates which milestones have been reached, or *not* reached as the case may be!

There are a number of major steps that need to be constantly thought about:

> ➢ Step 1: Look for the potential problems.
> ➢ Step 2: Decide what or who may be affected.
> ➢ Step 3: Evaluate the effects and decide whether existing precautions are sufficient or more should be done.
> ➢ Step 4: Write down your findings.
> ➢ Step 5: Review your assessment on a preset date and revise it if necessary.

Do not be over-complicated. Checking the various services is common sense, but necessary if you are not to have any major surprises.

The following questions should also be asked on a regular basis:

> ➢ Why is this job/task/service done? Does it need to be continued? Can the need for it be avoided?
> ➢ How is it done? Why is it done this way? Can a better way be found?
> ➢ When is it done? Why is it done then? Can a better time be found?

> ➢ Where is it done? Why is it done there? Can a better place be found?
> ➢ Who does it? Why is it done by him/her/them? Would another person/group be better, and perhaps cheaper?
> ➢ Where are we now?
> ➢ How did we get here?
> ➢ Where are we going?
> ➢ Where should we be going?
> ➢ How are we going to get there?

Equally so, users/customers should:

> ➢ be aware of what the information service can do
> ➢ identify their information problems
> ➢ communicate them to the information staff and be willing to discuss them
> ➢ give feedback on the quality and/or timeliness of the information services to the information staff
> ➢ keep the information staff aware of changing subject interests
> ➢ involve the information service in projects which have information implications.

So there is a need to be in constant dialogue with all users of the service, and with all colleagues. The people who are carrying out the jobs should know if a service is effective, and everyone should be encouraged to discuss if the tasks/jobs/services need altering. This is why the service plan needs to be revisited and revised. You have to develop a sixth sense in order to know whether the whole truth is being disclosed, or whether the speaker is merely saying what he/she thinks the listener wants to hear! More of this is discussed in Chapter 7.

Introducing new services

It is essential that the service plan should be revised *before* a new service is introduced. At the beginning of this chapter we posed a number of questions which should be asked when a new technology-based service is introduced. You need to be thinking about these questions at all stages of the development of the new service.

Also, before the business plan is compiled to introduce a new service, negotiations should have taken place with all potential users, and most importantly with the staff who will be involved in delivering the service. This will ensure that there are no surprises awaiting anyone when the service is finally introduced.

When the business plan is compiled to introduce a new service, it should include the costs of the service, the necessary hardware, software, furniture, space and location, opening hours, and the training costs for staff and users. In Chapter 5 of *Becoming a successful intrapreneur* (see Appendix A) we give many examples of new services but also remind you about the impact of new services on the remainder of the services.

Regular communication with users and staff will be the responsibility of those assigned to implement the new service. In Chapter 2 of *First Steps in Management* (see Appendix A), Beryl Morris gives some excellent tips on the subject of communication. She says that 'organizations invest a lot of effort into telling staff of changes and developments, less into ensuring that the staff have really understood the message.' The same applies to communicating with users. Beryl also goes on to say that 'the principles of effective communication, whether with groups or individuals, are as follows.

Communication should be:

➢ clear
➢ correct
➢ concise
➢ courteous
➢ consistent.

From this chapter you will know:

➢ how often your service plan should be revised
➢ questions to ask to help in your continuous assessment of services
➢ how to get users to tell you about the services
➢ what to do before, during and after introducing new services.

Chapter 7
Winning other people over

In this chapter you will find out:

> how to persuade others to participate in your service plan
> about the question of ownership
> about winning over management, staff, customers and suppliers.

As we noted in Chapter 3, in order to achieve success for your information service, it is essential to persuade users and others to participate in the compilation of the service plan. To encourage these various people to be involved, there are many ways in which the information services staff can offer their services, professional advice and guidance. The following ideas may be considered:

> You could help users to set up small systems for handling the information that they need for immediate reference within their own sections, departments or even as individuals.
> You could ask people from user departments to give talks about their personal work plans to the information staff.
> You could organize regular visits by information staff to meetings of user departments, to talk about the services and get feedback from the users.
> You could plan to assign members of the information staff to other departments for a particular project, to get to know particular areas of the organization. Staff members in turn may share knowledge with colleagues in the information service on their return. This has been very successful in some organizations and in various govern-

ment departments, ensuring long-term collaboration and cooperation.

➤ Regular contact, through the monitoring of any service level agreements that may exist, will ensure that both the information staff and the users are kept aware of developments, including planned developments taking place in various areas of the organization. If no service level agreement exists, then you will need to set up a programme to ensure regular contact with your users to discuss the service plan and any developments.

➤ You can be aware of the major areas of work of the organization, and offer the help of the information services.

The question of ownership

One of the most difficult tasks for the information service is to build up enough confidence in users and the management so that they will think of the information service as 'their' information service – in other words, to create a climate of ownership or stakeholding so that all areas of the organization will want the information service to succeed in order to be able to help them succeed in their own jobs.

Pursuing some of the ideas above will help, but you and other members of the information staff will need to be able to think on your feet and articulate sound arguments, and to be able to present ideas with conviction! There are several ways to do this.

Structuring a persuasive argument

You need to be constantly ready with a persuasive argument, particularly when developing and presenting your service plan. You and other information staff need to:

➤ ask questions to be able to identify the other person's information needs

➤ describe your proposition and show how it will meet that need

➤ support your claims by offering evidence which is relevant to the other person's interests

➤ welcome objections – they are a sign of interest

> allow interruptions –other people will not listen until they have had their say
> never argue – you can win the argument but lose the customer
> ask for a decision – offer positive alternatives.

Seeking success: steps in successful negotiation

Not everyone enjoys negotiating, but to become more proficient and successful you must be well prepared. Learn how to define your objectives clearly. Decide which are negotiable, gather information and get to know your 'opponent'. Not everyone shares the same enthusiasm for information as you do. Some points to remember:

> discuss; listen; exchange information; establish priorities; seek and give information; avoid argument
> listen for signals that are signs of movement; be willing to reciprocate
> make a conditional proposal – address your opponent's interests, incorporating concessions that have been signalled
> bargain – exchange concessions: 'If you do this, then we will do that'
> secure agreement and close firmly
> follow up swiftly any agreements and proposals made.

Winning people over

Management

You have set the scene to open discussion about the compilation of the service plan with various users, but you need to ensure that your management know what you are doing. You do not want to start off by upsetting the management. First you need to have a draft service plan that you can discuss with your manager. Assuming that there are no objections, you can then start to negotiate with the managers or supervisors of the various user groups. We have found that in practice, once you get this process moving, then the managers of the various sections will want to discuss their own service plans with the information service on a regular basis to ensure that they get the type and quality of service needed to enable their plans to succeed.

Staff

Equally important is for you to win over all your colleagues in the information service, to ensure that everyone is comfortable with the proposed service plans and that no one feels threatened, either because they do not understand what is being proposed or, worse still, they do not feel trained or competent enough to carry out the proposed work. Remember: communicating often and clearly is essential. Do not let other colleagues suffer because you think they understand what is being proposed.

Again, regular meetings will ensure that all staff are given the opportunity to participate in the development of the service plan. Any staff training will also need to be added and costed into the plans, with appropriate timescales.

If there are important projects to be carried out, such as a new service, a website, a newsletter etc, then you and the staff who are to carry out the work need to be fully appraised of the details that are essential.

For some extra details you may wish to refer to two other titles in the same series as this title (see Appendix A):

> ➢ *Making project management work for you* by Liz MacLachlan spells out the many and varied milestones in a project and emphasizes that the success of any project is very dependent on each and every step being completed successfully.
> ➢ *First steps in management* by Beryl Morris offers highly practical advice on managing effective teams and delivery of quality and service.

Customers

If you are now happy that you have won over your management and your colleagues, you will need to ensure that your customers/users are on board and are enthusiastic and willing, especially if they have to pay for the use of the information services. Perhaps the customers are the most difficult group to win over. Remember the advice we gave you at the beginning of the chapter about developing a persuasive argument. You also need to be fully aware of what is happening in the outside world of the information industry. By going to conferences and exhibitions, such as the annual Online Conference in London, and by constantly reading, you will know what is happening and can bring these new ideas to your users.

If you are at the stage of revamping your information service, or starting a completely new service, you will need to 'sell' the service. In *Putting marketing ideas into action* and in *Becoming a successful intrapreneur* (see Appendix A) you will find many ideas on how to get the message across to your customers. But remember that the users do not know what is really happening in the information industry, and that you have to act as a navigator to get the ideas across to them and help them appreciate that you are trying to keep them up to date in their own specialisms.

You will need to ensure that the terms you use every day when describing the various services do not confuse your users. You may have to define the terminology very carefully. For example, if you talk about serials, will your customer know you mean magazines or journals? And if you talk about a loan, will the user really know this means you have the right to ask for it back for another user? If you are looking for a glossary to define these terms, then British Standard 5408 is a good starting point (see Appendix A). We also have added a glossary at the end of this book (see Appendix C) to help you start a glossary of your own. You will certainly need your words and phrases defined if you set up a service level agreement between your users and the information service.

Continuing dialogue is essential, and it follows that you, and indeed all the information service staff, must give continual feedback and information to the users, because development in the information industry continues at such a high speed. The world wide web went from being an interesting sideline to an essential information tool within a very short space of time.

If there are any difficulties in the provision of the services, there need to be ways established for communicating these to the users. Thanks to this constant dialogue in customer care, the users will be willing to listen and comment honestly on any service plans or future projects for developing the information services.

Suppliers

Your role is now reversed from being the information supplier to being the customer. Think of all the steps in the process of a service being delivered to you, and ensure that your suppliers know what you want to achieve in your service plan. This way there are no surprises for you or them. The suppliers will welcome involvement, and will point out any problems they see, and many will, because of their experience, be able to help you.

In this chapter you:

➤ will know that it is essential to include everyone in developing your plan of work – management, colleagues, staff, customers and suppliers
➤ will know how essential it is to keep all communications lines open
➤ should be able to persuade others to participate in your service plan using sound debate and arguments
➤ should have a better idea of the question of ownership of who does what.

Chapter 8
Using your service plan to create a strategic position in your organization

In this chapter you will find out why you must:

➢ ensure that you have identified the key points in your service plan
➢ know how to communicate them to the management and users
➢ know the audience who will receive the service plan
➢ know the planning horizons
➢ have established good sources of information for future planning rounds
➢ be aware of the requirements for a successful service plan
➢ understand the reasons for developing a service plan
➢ know why your information service is regarded as central to the success of the organization.

Putting a service plan together requires you to translate your thoughts about how you are going to plan your information service, and how it will perform, into a format that is largely dictated by the requirements of your organization and the expectations of your users.

Whilst most service plans or business plans share a similar structure and contain similar information, your service plan will be distinguished by those characteristics that are unique to your business, be it an academic, legal, finance, special or public library and information service.

Just as each person's CV differs because it reflects the particular work experience of that individual, so each service plan will differ. But the format makes it instantly recognizable as a service plan. So you can use your service plan to create a strategic position in your particular organization that lines up with other plans of sections or departments within the organization. If other sections or departments do not have a service plan, then perhaps yours will inspire them.

Key points

You will need to examine a number of key points in developing the service plan. A well-developed, well-conceived plan can take from two to nine months to produce. In the preceding chapters we have shown how you need to communicate with various groups of people to ensure that you are producing a service plan that meets all needs. By doing this you are demonstrating that the information service is *central* to the organization and not just an 'add-on' which can be 'deleted' if times are hard. Over the past decade or so, there have been too many instances where a chief executive officer is looking for savings and at a stroke closes the information service. You can avoid going the same way by ensuring that your service plan shows the following key points:

Knowing your audience or user/customer groups

Who are you writing the service plan for? Your end-users will have different needs and expectations from your chief executive officer. Each group will view your service plan differently. But in the many discussions which you will have had over the preceding months, you will have identified:

- ➢ the main information needs of the organization and the staff
- ➢ the costs involved in providing these needs, including the equipment and any special external supplier organizations which you may need to use
- ➢ the financial forecasts
- ➢ the services and proposed services
- ➢ the customers, users and the potential users
- ➢ the necessary training of staff and users
- ➢ the publicity and marketing that will be needed
- ➢ any projects, either ongoing or new, and their component parts
- ➢ the timescales and milestones involved, and the planning horizons
- ➢ the competitors
- ➢ the key people who will be involved in the delivery of various tasks.

All these should appear in your service plan and in the executive summary that you need to produce to ensure that even the busiest chief executive will want to read it.

By producing the service plan you are showing that the information service can be, and will continue to be, a major stakeholder in the success of the organization. You will have identified the priority areas of work, taking on board all the requirements of the various user groups.

The planning horizon

During discussions you will have gained enough knowledge to know how far your planning horizon should extend. If, for instance, your organization works on forecasting activities and budgets over a three-year cycle, then you will need to work to this timescale. It is no use producing a service plan that runs contrary to that of the main organization, because you may find that you have not forecasted ahead sufficiently. Because the information service is, or should be, technology-based, you will have had an in-depth discussion with your organization's technology section – unless of course that is part of the information service.

The type of business

Your particular organization will define your activities. If you are the information service of a government department or agency, you will be working towards your department's goals and core business. If you are a special information service for a legal organization, you will be specializing in legal information as your core business. Likewise, you could be working for a tax company, or a company specializing in employment law. If you are in an academic learning centre, then you will specialize in the major subject taught at your institution.

But the main objective is to *understand* the core business and stay at least one step ahead of the users or customers.

Sources of information

During all your discussions with users, management or suppliers, you will have amassed a great deal of information from different sources. Consider how you can reduce the time and effort required to analyse your ideas for when you are revising or updating your service plan.

Again this will demonstrate to your colleagues and management that you are business-like in your approach.

Requirements for success

During the creation of the service plan, you need to be able to set yourself up for success by taking a realistic look at the internal and external conditions of the organization, and most importantly the information industry. So you need to have a system in place to enable you to make reasonable predictions about the future – for example, in the way the converging technologies can assist your users to obtain easy and cost-effective access to the information they need.

You will also need to understand the evolving needs of the organization, and to know the movers and shakers within the organization and even those external to it. No vibrant organization stays static for long because, in this day and age, those that cannot make quick, well-judged decisions will find that others have overtaken them. We can see how organizations outside what was once thought to be the information industry territory have moved in and taken over these areas of work. There is rarely any going back to the status quo.

In Chapter 2 we warned about competitors. You should take heed and build this factor into your service plan. Do not try to hide anything from your management, because sooner or later someone may start to ask awkward questions, so it is better for you to be seen to be pointing out the competitors.

In the same chapter we also pointed to some of the problems with service plans and why they fail. You should enjoy creating the service plan, because it will contain exciting projects and developments that you want to fulfil. At the same time, it is worth repeating that your service plan may be weak because it lacks:

➢ realism
➢ flexibility
➢ faith
➢ precision.

If so, it will not convince anyone, and you may find your information service being subject to unwanted close scrutiny. This warning should be taken seriously!

The final presentation of the service plan

Well, now is the acid test: will the service plan succeed and gain the recognition that you had hoped for? Remember that the service plan has been developed for two main reasons:

> ➢ to document important information which is relevant, analysed, with key decisions and action points
> ➢ to demonstrate the business approach by the information service to furnish users, management, suppliers and others with knowledge of the services to be provided.

You will need to produce an executive summary that can be available for use by the chief executive, who will no doubt need to incorporate this into his or her overall service plan. All well-developed service plans should suggest key sections for you to pull out in the executive summary. The executive summary can also be used as part of the publicity and marketing effort of the information service.

In conclusion, hopefully you will:

> ➢ have ensured that you have identified the key points in your service plan
> ➢ know how to communicate them to the management and users
> ➢ know the audience who will receive the service plan
> ➢ know the planning horizons
> ➢ have established good sources of information for future planning rounds
> ➢ be aware of the requirements for a successful service plan
> ➢ understand the reasons for developing a service plan
> ➢ know why your information service can be regarded as central to the success of the organization.

Further reading

No descriptions of these items have been given where titles are self explanatory.

Chapter 1   Why you need a service plan

Bangs, D, *The business planning guide,* Upstart Publishing Co, 1995, 7th edn, ISBN 1574100998.

A basic resource written in an informal style with worksheets, a glossary, reference list and 'entrepreneur's resource guide'. Also includes business plans for fictional businesses.

Kahrs, K (ed) *Business plans handbook: a compilation of actual business plans developed by small businesses throughout North America,* Gale Research, 1994, ISBN 0810392224.

A basic resource made up almost entirely of 33 actual service, product, high tech, non-profit, virtual reality and other business plans. Does not include worksheets. Includes a glossary of small business terms and a resource list of 750 Small Business Development Centers in the United States. Has an extensive bibliography of resources for business owners.

McKee, B, *Planning library service,* Library Association Publishing, 1989, ISBN 0851574246.

Now getting a little old, but has some useful advice.

Pantry, S and Griffiths, P, *The complete guide to service level agreements,* Library Association Publishing, 1997, ISBN 1856042391.

Service level agreements are increasingly being used in the information and library sector. This book covers all aspects of developing, negotiating and specification writing. It also includes chapters on managing customers and suppliers.

Pantry, S and Griffiths, P, *Becoming a successful intrapreneur,* Library Association Publishing, 1998, ISBN 1856042928.

Information services of all kinds need to be proactive within their institution by using entrepreneurial skills internally, marketing themselves vigorously and promoting their value. This book shows how with examples, worksheets and cross-sectoral studies.

Pantry, S and Griffiths, P, *Your successful LIS career*, Library Association Publishing, 1999, ISBN 1856043290.

How to formulate a career plan.

Pinchot, G, *Intrapreneuring: why you don't have to leave the corporation to become an entrepreneur*, Harper and Row, 1985 (new edition due September 2000, ISBN 1576750825).

One of the successful promoters of intrapreurship.

Pinson, L and Jinnett, J, *Anatomy of a business plan*, Dearborn Trade, 4th edn, 1999, ISBN 1574101277.

A basic resource written in an informal style. Includes worksheets, definitions, and contact information. Also includes a business plan for a fictional tool and dye firm.

Scammell, A (ed) *Handbook of special librarianship and information work*, Aslib, 1997, 7th edn, ISBN 0851423981.

Covers a wide range of information services.

Chapter 2 The contents of a service plan

Allen, B, *InfoMapper instructor's guide,* for use with InfoMapper software (but sold separately), Information Management Press, Inc, PO Box 19166, Washington, DC 20036, USA, ISBN 0960640835.

Burk, C F Jr and Horton, F W Jr, *InfoMap: the complete guide to discovering corporate information resources*, Prentice Hall, 1988. Now available from Information Management Press, Inc, PO Box 19166, Washington, DC 20036, USA, ISBN 013464476.

Business PlanWrite. Software to guide you through the creation of a plan, available at:

http://www.brs-inc.com/pwrite.html

Central Computer and Telecommunications Agency (CCTA) UK, *PRINCE – PRojects IN Controlled Environments.*

A project management method developed by the CCTA, concerned with the organization, management and control of projects. It was originally devised for managing information technology projects but has been developed into PRINCE 2, a general project management system suitable for a wide range of public sector and other projects.

Cohen, W, *Model business plans for product businesses*, J Wiley, 1995, ISBN 0471030287.

A basic guide to business plan writing for product businesses, including worksheets and 12 complete sample product business plans.

Corrall, S, *Strategic planning for library and information services*, Aslib, 1994, ISBN 0851423302.

Covello, J and Hazelgren, B J, *The complete book of business plans: simple steps to writing a powerful business plan*, Sourcebooks Trade, 1994, ISBN 0942061411.

Covello, J and Hazelgren, B J, *Your first business plan: a simple question and answer format design to help you write your own plan*, Sourcebooks Trade, 3rd edn, 1998, ISBN 1570712190.

Deloitte and Touche Growth Company Services, *Writing an effective business plan*, 2nd ed, 1999, available at:
http://www.us.deloitte.com/growth
Provides section-by-section advice for writing a business plan. Suitable for executives of both new and established companies who need an effective business plan to secure financing, attract senior managers and directors, introduce the company to prospective partners, or simply to use as a compass for the company's mission and goals.

Department of Trade and Industry, *Business planning – a quick guide for chief executives and management teams in small and medium sized companies*, URN 99/959, August 1994 (reprinted March 1999). Free of charge and available from DTI Publications Orderline, Admail 528, London SW1W 8YT, UK. Tel: +44 (0)870 150 2500, Fax: (0)870 1500 2333, e-mail: dtipubs@echristian.co.uk.

Hart, K, *Putting marketing ideas into action*, Library Association Publishing, 1998, ISBN 1856041824.

Hildebrand, C, *Information mapping: guiding principles*, *CIO: the magazine for Information Executives*, July 1995, **8** (18), 60–4.

Horton, F W Jr, *Mapping corporate information resources* (three part series of articles in the *International Journal of Information Management*, 1988, **8**, 249–54; 1989, **9**, 19–24; 1989, **9**, 91–5.

Horton, F W Jr, Infomapping, *The Electronic Library*, February 1991, **9** (1), 17–19.

Horton, F W Jr, *The information management workbook: IRM made simple*, revised and updated third edition, loose-leaf 3 ring binder, 400 + pages, Information Management Press, Inc, PO Box 19166, Washington, DC 20036, USA, ISBN 0960640800.

infoUSA.com, *Planning your business: preparing to write your business plan*, Toolkit suggesting headings and key issues for your plan, available at:
http://www.infousa.com/toolkit/home/text/PO2_4001.htm

Journal of Knowledge Management, IFS International Ltd, Wolseley Business Park, Kempston, Bedford MK42 7PW.
Useful to keep checking for the latest on knowledge management and planning.

Kravitt, G I, *Creating a winning business plan: a no-time-for nonsense guide to starting a business and raising capital*, Probus Publishing, 1993, ISBN 1557384711.
Assumes some business background. Information is presented in a question-and-answer format with checklists to follow. Now out of print.

Lannon, R, *InfoMapper project manager's guide*, for use with InfoMapper software (but sold separately), Information Management Press, Inc, PO Box 19166, Washington, DC 20036, USA, ISBN 0960640851.

Library Association, *Delivering quality library and information services: LA Training Package*, Library Association Publishing, 1996, ISBN 1856042146.

Library Association, *Developing business/service plans for a competitive future: LA Training Package*, Library Association Publishing, 1997, ISBN 1856042731.

McKeever, M, *How to write a business plan*, Nolo Press, 2000, 5th edn, ISBN 0873375440.

Basic resource presented in an informal style. Three sample business plans and an extensive list of resources. Does not include worksheets.

MIT Enterprise Forum®, Inc, *Business plan resource guide,* available at:

http://web.mit.edu/entforum/www/Business_Plans/bplans.html

O'Hara, P D, *The total business plan: how to write, rewrite, and revise,* J Wiley, 1995, 2nd edn, ISBN 0471078298.

Assumes some knowledge of business plan writing. Includes a 3½ in. diskette with pro forma statement, income statement, cash flow analysis, and profit and loss statement on Lotus spreadsheets. Also includes two full sample business plans.

Pantry, S and Griffiths, P, *The complete guide to service level agreements,* Library Association Publishing, 1997, ISBN 1856042391.

Service level agreements are increasingly being used in the information and library sector. This book covers all aspects of developing, negotiating and specification writing. It also includes chapters on managing customers and suppliers.

Small Business Administration, USA, available at:

http://www.sba.gov/starting

From SBA Web Site, select 'Starting your Business', then select 'Business Plans'. Useful basic resource available on the World Wide Web. Includes worksheets and SBA and other government agency contact information. Does not include a sample plan.

Chapter 3 Why go it alone? Involving others in your service plan

Abell, A (ed) *The information professional of the 21st century: report by TFPL,* 1997.

Looks at the skills required for those working in information services of the future.

Bluck, R, *Team management,* Library Association Publishing, 1996, ISBN 1856041670.

International Business Machines Inc (IBM), *The net result: social inclusion in the information society. Report of the National Working Party on*

Social Inclusion (INSINC), IBM United Kingdom Ltd, 1997, also available at:

http:www.uk.ibm.com/comm/community/uk117.html

Kirby, J et al, *Empowering the information user*, Library Association Publishing, 1997, ISBN 1856042529.

Identifying user groups and their needs.

Lyon, J, Personal development: understanding knowledge, *Information World Review*, May 1997, 24–5.

Masterton, A, *Getting results with time management*, Library Association Publishing, 1997, ISBN 1856042375.

A useful book specially written for those working in library and information services.

Pantry, S, Whither the information professional?: challenges and opportunities. The cultivation of information professional for the new Millennium. Presented at the Aslib Electronics and Multimedia Groups Annual Conference, 14–16 May 1997, *Aslib Proceedings*, June 1997, **49** (6), 170–2.

Pantry, S (ed) *Building community information networks: strategies and experiences*, Library Association Publishing, 1999, ISBN 1-85604-337–1.

Pantry, S and Griffiths, P, *Becoming a successful intrapreneur*, Library Association Publishing, 1998, ISBN 1856042928.

Information services of all kinds need to be proactive within their institution by using entrepreneurial skills internally, marketing themselves vigorously and promoting their value. This book shows how with examples, worksheets and cross-sectoral studies.

Ryan, P (ed) *Time for change: threat or opportunity?*, Circle of State Librarians, 1997.

Chapter 4 Your personal plan – personal and professional development plans

Covey, S R, *The 7 habits of highly successful people: powerful lessons in personal change*, Franklin Covey Co, 1989. Reprinted Simon and Schuster UK, 1999, ISBN 0684858398.

Department for Education and Employment (DfEE), *Mentoring for work-based training*, Good Practice Series: GPS/WD2/1/99, April 1999, ISBN 0855229942.

Available from DfEE, Quality and Performance Improvement Division, Level 3 North, Moorfoot Sheffield S1 4PQ, UK. Tel: 0845 602 2260.

Ditzler, J (2000) *Your best year yet! A proven method for making your next 12 months your most successful ever*, Warner, ISBN 0446675474.

European Commission DGXIII/E-4 Telematics Application Programme, *The EUROIEMASTERS: the information engineering professional*. Details from: European Commission DGXIII/E-4, Euroforum. 10 Rue Robert Stumper, L-2557 Luxembourg.

There is continuing pressure for the Information Engineering Professional (IEP) to keep her/his skills and knowledge constantly updated. The EUROIEMASTERS Syllabus offers IEPs opportunities to extend and develop their knowledge and skills. The brochure is useful to identify the skills needed.

Référentiel des métiers-types et compétences des professionnels de l'information et documentation, Édition definitive, Paris, ADBS, 1998.

The following websites give useful information

Australian Library and Information Assocation, *Career development kit*, available at:

http://www.alia.org.au/publications/career.kit.html

Institute of Information Scientists, *Criteria for information science*, available at:

http://www.iis.org.uk/membership/Criteria.html

Library Association, *Framework for continuing professional development* (CPD), available at:

http://www.la-hq.org.uk/directory/training/training_dev_4.html

Special Library Association, *Competencies for special librarians of the 21st century*, available at:

http://www.sla.org/professional/comp.html

Chapter 5 Evaluating and monitoring your service plan

Abbott, C, *Performance measurement in library and information services*, Aslib, 1994, ISBN 0851423299.

Aslib, *Performance measures and metrics*, Aslib, 1999– .

Bennett, D, Quality assurance: two day course 26–27 June 1991: report, Aslib, 1991.

Bloor, I P, *Performance indicators and decision support systems for libraries: a practical application of 'keys to success'*, British Library Research and Development Department, 1991 (British Library Research Papers 93), ISBN 0712332510.

British Standard BS ISO 11620: 1998, *Information and documentation. Library performance indicators*, BSI, 1998.

Brockman, J (ed) *Quality management and benchmarking in the information sector: results of recent research.* (British Library Research and Innovation Report 47), Bowker-Saur, 1997, ISBN 1857391896.

Griffiths, J-M and King, D W, *A manual on the evaluation of information centers and services (manuel pour l'evaluation des centres et services d'information)* [S.l.] [AGARD], Distributed by the American Institute of Aeronautics and Astronautics, Technical Information Service, Paris: distributed by NATO, 1991, AGARDograph no.310.

Martin, D, *Total quality management*, LITC, Library and Information Briefings 45, 1993.

Office for Arts and Libraries, *Keys to Success: performance indicators for public libraries*, Library Information Series no.18, HMSO, 1990, ISBN 014300488.
A manual of performance measures and indicators developed by King Research Ltd.

Performance indicators for university libraries: a practical guide, Standing Conference of National and University Libraries, Advisory Committee, 1992, (SCONUL Doc 92/204), ISBN 0900210117.

Ward, S et al, *Library performance indicators and library management tools*, European Commission, DG XIII-E3, Office for Official Publications of the European Communities, 1995, ISBN 9282749010.

Chapter 6 'Well, we did a service plan once!' Ensuring that your service plan stays alive!

Kirby, J et al, *Empowering the information user*, Library Association Publishing, 1997, ISBN 1856042529.

Laamanen, I, Quality management in the information service centre of the FIOH, in *Health information management: what strategies?* Bakker, S (ed), 57–60, 1997, Kluwer Academic Publishers.

Library Association, *Delivering quality library and information services: LA Training Package*, Library Association Publishing, 1996, ISBN 1856042146.

McLaughlin, H, *The entrepreneur's guide to building a better business plan: a step by step approach*, J Wiley, 1992.
Assumes some business background. Does not include worksheets. Includes a bibliography and a chapter called 'When your business plan fails'. Includes two actual business plans used throughout book to illustrate aspects of the business plan writing process.

Morris, B, *First steps in management*, Library Association Publishing, 1996, ISBN 1856041832.
Now out of print but perhaps can be borrowed on interlibrary loan.

Chapter 7 Winning other people over

British Standards Institution, BS 5408:1976 *Glossary of documentation terms*, BSI, 1976.

Foster, A, Convincing others of the need to change, *Library manager*, 2, 1994, 20–1.

Hart, K, *Putting marketing ideas into action*, Library Association Publishing, 1999, ISBN 1856041824.
Excellent guide to involving others in your marketing and other plans.

MacLachlan, L, *Making project management work for you*, Library Association Publishing, 1996, ISBN 1855042030.

Morris, B, *First steps in management*, Library Association Publishing, 1996, ISBN 1856041832.
Now out of print but perhaps can be borrowed on interlibrary loan.

Pantry, S and Griffiths, P, *Becoming a successful intrapreneur*, Library Association Publishing, 1998, ISBN 1856042928.

Information services of all kinds need to be proactive within their institution by using entrepreneurial skills internally, marketing themselves vigorously and promoting their value. This book shows how, with examples, worksheets and cross-sectoral studies.

Chapter 8 Using your service plan to create a strategic position in your organization

Coote, H and Batchelor, B, *How to market your library service effectively*, Aslib, 2nd edn, 1998, ISBN 0851423965.

de Sáez, E E, *Marketing concepts for libraries and information services*, Library Association Publishing, 1993, ISBN 0851574483.

Hamilton, F, *Infopromotion*, Gower, 1990, ISBN 0566055775.

Library Association, *Marketing library and information services: LA Training Package*, Library Association Publishing, 1997, ISBN 185604274X.

Ormes, S and Dempsey, L (eds) *The Internet, networking and the public library*, Library Association Publishing, 1997, ISBN 1856042022.

St Clair, G, *Customer service in the information environment*, Bowker-Saur, 1994, ISBN 1857390040.

St Clair, G, *Power and influence enhancing information services within the organisation*, Bowker-Saur, 1994, ISBN 1857390989.

Other websites of interest

MIT Enterprise Forum®, Inc, 28 Carleton Street, Building E32-336, Cambridge, MA 02139, USA. Tel: + 1 617 253 0015; Fax: +1 617 258 0532; e-mail: mitef@mit.edu.
http: //web.mit.edu/entforum

Pinchot, G, The Intrapreneur pages – The ten commandments; Are you an Intrapreneur?, available at:
http://www.geogroup.net/TI/Innovate/Pinchot/

Software

InfoMapper software package, IBM Compatible Standalone PC

Version (Release 1.2 Mod. 1) User Manual ISBN 0960640843, LAN also available, as well as French, Spanish and German language IBM Compatible PC versions. Information Management Press, Inc, PO Box 19166, Washington, DC 20036, USA.

Appendix B
Service plan template

We suggest the headings below as a guide.

Remember that many plans are much too long. Be succinct. Structure your plan with plenty of headings and a good index. Say what you intend to achieve, indicate broadly how you intend to achieve it, and how you will know when you have achieved it. If you must explain, leave the detail to another document or an annex.

NB Check the appropriate chapters in this book for advice and guidance.

Suggested headings

Name of information service

1 **Aims and objectives**: What your organization wants the information service to achieve.
2 **A statement of your services**, including number of staff and grades.
3 **Standards laid down** for the services.
4 **User needs** – short, medium and long term.
5 **New services**: development and timescales.
6 **Materials/acquisitions**, including computerized information, journals etc. Indicate committed costs, eg subscriptions, standing orders and other costs.
7 **Statement on equipment currently held**, expected date and cost of replacement. Include details of equipment that you know will be required during the planning period.
8 **Training costs** for staff and users.
9 **Building costs**, including rents and maintenance costs.
10 **Maintenance costs** for software and hardware.
11 **Communications costs**, including telephone, fax, Internet and post.

12 **Promotion and publicity costs.**

13 **Binding and repair costs.**

14 **Consumables costs,** which should include both general expenses such as computer stationery and specialist materials such as date labels or the cost of producing borrowers' cards.

15 **Collection development policy:** you will find that your subject classification scheme makes a good starting point for a statement of your subject specialisms.

16 **Retirement policy** for materials held in the information service.

17 **Archiving and conservation plans** for items held permanently such as company annual reports and accounts.

18 **Emergency procedures** for staff, users and also materials and equipment.

19 **Costing the plan,** including the timescale for spending the budget.

20 **Competition,** both within and outside the organization.

21 **A glossary of definitions** used in the service plan, to avoid any misunderstandings.

22 **Index.**

Appendix C
Glossary

We have included words and terms used not only in this book but elsewhere in the compilation of service plans and budgets, including some fairly technical accounting terms which may be of assistance. An asterisk (*) denotes use in public-sector organizations.

Accommodation

Costs of rents, rates, maintenance, furniture, heating, lighting, water etc.

Accounting

The formal, systematic measurement and recording of financial inputs and outputs to ensure adherence to financial plans and budgets on a continuous basis and the presentation to the fiscal authority of a year-end balance for taxation purposes.

Accounting officer*

An officer appointed to sign accounts within his/her responsibility and by virtue of that duty, additionally being a witness to deal with questions arising from the accounts.

Accounts

Statements of monetary transactions with the resulting balance.

Accruals

The concept of accruals accounting and budgeting requires income and expenditure to be recognized when they are earned or incurred, not when they are received or paid out. Under this system, a libary order would be shown as a cost in the month when the order was placed, not when the invoice was received.

Agreement

A generic term for a legally binding undertaking between buyer and supplier, in terms of obligations, relationships and responsibilities between them – what is commonly described as a contract. In its simplest form an agreement can be verbal. The more usual approach is to make it in writing, using a standard document or a specifically prepared document (often also described as a contract). Once an agreement has been made there is a commitment.

Allocated costs

Costs which have been allocated or divided between departments or services on whose behalf the items were purchased, eg equipment shared by a number of departments/services.

Ambit (of a Vote) ★

The description in the UK Government's Supply Estimate, or in a Supplementary Estimate, of the purposes for which a provision is made. The ambit appears in a Schedule to the Appropriation Act, and Parliament authorizes specific sums of money to each ambit for spending only on matters within that ambit.

Analysis of Public Expenditure (APEX) ★

A system operated by the Paymaster General's Office which records the expenditure and receipts of Government departments.

Appropriation Account ★

An end-of-year account of Government departments' spending of monies voted by Parliament which compares the Supply Estimate (down to subhead level, but not below) with actual payments made and receipts brought to account, and explains any substantial differences. An Appropriation Account is prepared for each Vote, audited and reported to Parliament.

Appropriation Act ★

The statutory authority which authorizes issues from the Consolidated Fund and appropriates all money granted by Parliament to some distinct use.

Appropriations in Aid ★

Receipts which, with the authority of Parliament, are used to finance some of the gross expenditure on the Vote, thus limiting the amount to be issued from the Consolidated Fund to the net Vote.

Approved list

Also known as a trade list or eligible list: a list of potential suppliers. See **Supplier appraisal**.

Approved supplier

See **Supplier appraisal**.

Audit

An investigation by an outside body, or a body external to the department being audited, into the cost-effectiveness of the services.

Balanced scorecard

A business management method devised by Robert Kaplan and David Norton that emphasizes strategic approaches and examines the customer, financial, process and learning perspectives of an organization's activities.

Bid

May also be known as a tender, quote or quotation. A supplier's offer to provide goods or services for a consideration in response to the buyer's enquiry or invitation to tender.

Bid appraisal

May also be known as bid (or tender) analysis, evaluation or assessment. The formal process of looking at suppliers' bids to identify which provides the best value for money.

Bid conditioning

A process whereby suppliers' bids are scrutinized for conformity with the enquiry documents, errors and omissions rectified, and any other points clarified, so that like-for-like appraisal of the bids can be made.

Breakeven month

The month in the analysis when the positive forecasted cash flow equates to the negative cumulative cash flow.

Budget

A summary of probable financial outlays and incomes over a specified period of time – the total outlay of money allocated for a specific purpose during a specified period.

Budgetary management

The sum of methods, techniques and events which contribute to the final outcomes from the allocation of resources.

Business Excellence Model

A business management method that examines a range of topics including, among others, people management, policy, strategy, customer satisfaction and impact on society. It uses the scores for each element to arrive at an overall rating for the organization. It was developed by the European Foundation for Quality Management and is championed in the UK by the British Quality Foundation.

Business strategy

The tactics adopted by an organization to ensure that its objectives are achieved in a finite future time period.

Capital costs

The costs of acquiring new equipment etc, making provision for depreciation. When equipment is leased, capital costs will comprise the rental and maintenance costs.

Capital expenditure *

Expenditure on new construction, land and extensions of, and alterations to, existing buildings, and the purchase of any other fixed assets (eg machinery and plant) – including vehicles – having an expected working life of more than one year. Also includes stocks, grants for capital purposes, and lending.

Cash flow

Income and expenditure. Measurement over a fixed period of time of monies received and spent by an organization. Positive (more cash in than out) is good, negative the opposite. Forecasting cash flow is an essential element of financial planning.

Cash limit *

The limit set by ministers on the amount of cash that can be spent on certain specified services during one financial year.

Charging

Putting a price on services. The amount charged in the public sector may be influenced as much by social considerations as by commercial factors.

Citizens' Charter

An initiative stemming from the endeavours of the UK Government's Efficiency Unit to improve public-sector services. The initiative became known as Service First before being absorbed into the Modernizing Government programme.

Class *

A group of Votes which broadly correspond to one of the departmental chapters in the Public Expenditure White Paper.

Client

A purchaser/customer of professional services or goods – term much used by consultants.

Close out

Action on the part of the buyer to review the contract file after completion of the work. The buyer ensures that all documents are up to date and that they properly reflect and record the detail of the case. A close-out report reviewing the case may be prepared, and this is the ideal time to complete and file a vendor rating on the supplier concerned.

Commitment

The result of formalizing an agreement by an act of acceptance. May also be used to describe the financial value of an agreement – the amount committed.

Common services costs

In large organizations, centrally provided services such as heat, light, cleaning and maintenance are allocated as overhead costs to departments on a predetermined basis, eg on floor space allocated.

Competitive tendering

Awarding contracts by the process of seeking competing tenders.

Consideration

A legal term used to describe the payment made for the goods or services provided by a supplier.

Consignment stocking

Stock items or lines held at the buyer's premises but owned by the supplier and not paid for until usage is replaced by the supplier. Alternatively, the supplier may hold the stock for the buyer's exclusive use.

Consolidated Fund ★

The Exchequer account into which are paid tax revenue, less repayments, and all other Exchequer receipts not specifically directed elsewhere. Issues from the Fund include those to meet Supply services shown in Supply Estimates.

Consolidated Fund Extra Receipts (CFER) ★

Receipts related to expenditure in the Supply Estimates which Parliament has not authorized to be used as Appropriations in Aid and are therefore surrendered to the Consolidated Fund.

Consumer

The person or body who makes use of a commodity or service. Food, drink, gas, water and electricity are obvious examples, but all products are consumed, eg books, education.

Contingencies Fund

A fund which can be used for urgent expenditure in anticipation of provision by Parliament becoming available. It is administered by Parliament under strict rules. Drawings on this fund must be repaid when Parliament has voted the additional sums required.

Contract

See **Agreement**. Often used to describe a standalone document setting out the terms of the agreement between buyer and seller, prepared to include specific conditions rather than the general conditions used in a standard purchase order.

Contracting out

An activity or even the work of a whole department may be contracted or subcontracted out to an outside supplier. Commonplace in commercial organizations. In the public sector the internal supplier can become an external supplier.

Control

A system to ensure that inputs and outputs are of a required value, volume and price.

Cost

Measurement of the amount of resources required to obtain a product or service.

Cost accounting

Sometimes called management accounting. The recording/controlling of all expenditures of an enterprise in order to facilitate control of separate functions.

Cost benefits

Cost saving, cost avoidance.

Cost centre ★

A location, person or item of equipment (or group of these such as a division, local office or workshop) for which costs may be ascertained and used for the purpose of cost control. Cost centres are usually organizational subdivisions of responsibility or budget centres.

Cost-effectiveness

The cheapest means of achieving defined objectives or obtaining maximum value for money.

Cost measurement

Determination of the total cost of product or service. This will include staff, materials and overheads.

Cost plus

Payment terms under which a supplier is reimbursed for actual (ascertained) costs plus an addition for profit, either an agreed fixed amount or a percentage of costs. See also **Firm price**.

Debriefing

The term used to describe the process of explaining to unsuccessful tenderers why they have not been awarded the business, to help suppliers improve their competitive performance.

Deliverables

A collective name for all those tangible things that the supplier or contractor is required to supply under the agreement. It includes goods or finished works, together with drawing, specifications and any other related documentation. It does not usually include intangibles such as warranties – these are commonly termed 'ongoing obligations'.

Depreciation

Usually includes capital costing. Provisions for depreciation should be at current values, not historical values.

Devolved budget

That part of an organization's financial resources allocated to a defined part of the business.

Economic classification ★

An analysis of public-sector accounting transactions according to their economic character. It is based on the classification used by the

Central Statistical Office for compiling the accounts of national income and expenditure.

Economic order quantity (EOQ)

The most cost-effective quantity to order when purchasing for stock.

End-user

The actual user of the goods and services purchased by the buyer, responsible for stating the requirement and often the specification.

Enquiry

Also known as invitation to tender. The buyer invites suppliers to bid for business, usually setting out the specification and terms and conditions. Enquiry documents comprise all those documents – specification terms and conditions etc – sent to suppliers to enable them to bid.

Estimates

Forecasted financial calculations needed to fund the operation of an organization, usually in a given year, though it can be within a longer time frame.

Evaluation

The process by which the value of something is determined or established. Could be personal or individual, collective or corporate, formal or informal. Measurement in non-concrete areas such as effectiveness, customer satisfaction, consumer choice etc.

Excess Vote *

Only submitted in the rare circumstances when voted provision for the year is exceeded without an adequate increase being approved through a Supplementary Estimate.

Expediting

An organized and sustained activity to monitor a supplier's progressive achievement with the object of achieving deliveries on time.

Expenditure

Money being spent in staff pay, acquisitions, running of services, capital, maintenance of stock and buildings etc.

Financial Information System (FIS) *

A computerized system used by the Treasury to monitor information about the flow of voted and some other expenditure.

Financial management

The theory and practice of raising monies and controlling funds. Includes accounting, costing, budgetary control etc.

Financial year ★

The year from 1 April of one year to 31 March of the next. See also **Fiscal year**.

Firm price/fixed price

The term 'firm price' is usually used to describe a price that will hold until altered under a variation-of-price clause. The term 'fixed price' is usually used to describe a price which will hold without variation throughout the life of an agreement, usually provided that there is no significant change to the detail of the agreement. Some users reverse these definitions and you should check carefully what is meant by these terms.

Fiscal year

The 12-month period for record-keeping, accounting or tax purposes. The fiscal year is not necessarily the calendar year.

Forecasting

May best be regarded as one of the skills essential to planning and budgeting. Projections of future market opportunities and demands, material prices, labour availability etc.

Full economic cost

The total costs incurred by the producer to deliver goods or services. This will include personnel, equipment, materials etc.

Government information and library service

Set up by a Government department or agency to serve its needs and in some cases give service to the public. Funded by the department or agency.

Grant ★

Money voted (ie granted) by Parliament to meet the services shown in Supply Estimates. Also used in individual subheads of supply estimates to describe an unrequited payment to an individual body in the private sector. See also **Subsidy**.

Grant-in Aid ★

A grant from voted monies to a particular organization or body where certain unexpected balances of the sums issued will not be liable for surrender to the Consolidated Fund at the end of the financial year.

Higher education libraries

Libraries principally in universities and university-related institutions, and centrally funded through that institution via a central funding council.

Human resources

The people available to an organization or department. They may be full or part-time, employed or subcontracted, and are also the skill and knowledge resources as well as physical resources.

Income generation

The development of products or services for sale to provide revenue (usually to help supplement the library and information services budget).

Information systems

Usually known as management information systems which give details of cash, performance etc.

Inspection

The process of examining products during manufacture or on completion to assess their conformation to specification.

Institute of Purchasing and Supply (IPS)

The professional body for people working in the purchasing and supply functions.

Intellectual property rights (IPR)

The legal rights relating to the ownership of inventions, designs, processes, techniques, drawings, specifications, technical information and knowhow. Copyright, patents and trademarks are forms of IPR.

Inventory

A term used to describe a listing of stock by item (line item). The total of stocks held may also be described as 'the inventory'.

Invitation to tender

Invitation to suppliers to bid. See also **Enquiry**.

Joined-up government

A phrase used in the UK to denote the need to develop links between related policy or information issues handled in separate Government departments, and where connections are therefore missing between parts of the same policy.

Just-in-time (JIT)

A way to avoid holding excess stocks developed primarily in manufacturing, involving the delivery of parts, materials, components etc, only at the time when they are required for processing, assembly etc. It requires certainty as to suppliers' performance if JTL – 'just too late' – is to be avoided.

Lead time

The period of time that is considered to be required between defined events – for example, between the placing of an order and the delivery of goods – usually expressed as a number of working days or weeks.

Letter of intent

A method by which the buyer advises a potential supplier of a future intention to place an order. Such letters (which may also be telexes or faxes) usually have an expiry date and often specify the conditions to be fulfilled before an order will be placed. They should be used with care to avoid commitments being entered into prematurely or unintentionally.

LISU

Library and Information Statistics Unit, University of Loughborough.

Main programme ★

One of 18 main functional programmes within the public expenditure survey – for instance, defence, housing, social security. Most main programmes are further subdivided into subprogrammes.

Management accounting

Sometimes called cost accounting. The recording and controlling of all the expenditures of an enterprise in order to facilitate control of separate activities.

Management information systems

A product of the application of information technology to a business and sometimes known as information systems, they give details of cash, performance and trends, statistical analysis etc.

Market testing

Checking the market place for the current costs of a product or service and making comparisons with in-house costs. The original meaning was determining the viability of a product or service before launching it on the market. In the public sector, the efficiency of a department in providing a service or performing an activity is measured against competing tenders from external sources.

Materials management

A term used to describe purchasing and supply activity, primarily developed in a manufacturing context and with an emphasis on materials handling, stock control and distribution.

Mission statement

A short statement of the intent of the organization or business.

Offer

See **Bid**.

National Audit Office ★

Officers of this department carry out the audit of every Appropriation Account other than that of their own department.

National Libraries

Nationally funded libraries that usually benefit from legal deposit of publications.

National Loans Fund ★

The Government's account with the Bank of England through which all Government borrowing transactions (including payment of debt interest) and most lending transactions are handled.

Net subhead ★

A net subhead is created when receipts are offset against expenditure in a specific subhead, rather than Appropriated in Aid of the Vote as a whole. In some cases the receipts equal the expenditure and only a token £1000 is shown to be voted.

New Library

New Library: The People's Network. A report published in October 1997 by the Library and Information Commission, which argues that libraries must be repositioned as the communications backbone of the information society if the UK is to be a dynamic and competitive force into the next millennium.

Non-public expenditure ⋆

About 25% of voted provision is excluded from the PES figures because it concerns intermediate transfers (eg to the National Insurance Fund and to local authorities) which score later when paid to the public. This avoids double counting.

One-person band or one-person library

A small library or information unit within an organization or business, usually run by one professional person.

Out-turn ⋆

Actual expenditure at the end of the financial year.

Overtime pay

Where a workgroup or workforce has strictly defined basic hours of work, additional hours worked, eg weekends, may be paid at higher than base rate.

Payment timing

Payments can be made in advance or in arrears, and must be made within specified times – 30 days, 60 days etc. Sometimes they are required to be made on the first day of the month.

Performance activity indicator

All performance is measurable, sometimes with more difficulty than others, particularly where a task cannot be speeded up. Other areas must then be examined such as cost control and cost reduction, quality improvement, lost time elimination. Agreement between the parties concerned on 'measures' is essential.

Performance target

This may be set for the whole organization, with the overall target being allocated by top departments and individuals. Targets should preferably be agreed between parties involved.

Plan of work

A statement to your users and management of what the information service (IS) or learning resource centre (LRC) is going to achieve in the forthcoming years. Your plan could take in two to three years.

Planning in libraries

Includes making all services work effectively, meeting user needs, ensuring that future requirements can be assessed, and that staff are aware of the changing needs of users and trained accordingly.

Planning, programming budgeting system (PPBS)

The budget proposals of the plans, the specified programmes with costings, inputs and outputs.

Post-tender negotiation (PTN)

Discussions with a supplier or suppliers after their offers have been received, with the aim of achieving improvements.

Present value

The value today of a future payment, or stream of payments, discounted at the specified discount rate.

Pricing

Setting a value on goods or services. The level must be pitched at a point determined by considerations of cost of production, demand and profitability.

PRINCE (PRojects IN Controlled Environments)

A project management method developed by the Central Computer and Telecommunications Agency, and concerned with the organization, management and control of projects. It was originally devised for managing information technology projects but has been developed into PRINCE 2, a general project management system suitable for a wide range of public-sector and other projects.

Profiling

When funds have been allocated to various programmes of the LIS, it will be necessary to forecast the spend over the forthcoming year, showing the amount of budget to be spent each month. It will show broadly what each activity costs at any given time. This includes all costs, including staff costs. It will also show committed expenditure for the rest of the financial year.

Programme ★

See **Main programme**.

Public Accounts Committee ★

An all-party Select Committee of the House of Commons which is empowered to enquire into the financial administration of Government departments and examine their accounts. The Committee reports its findings to Parliament.

Public Expenditure Survey (PES) *

The Government's annual review of public expenditure for three years ahead.

Public Expenditure Survey Committee *

An interdepartmental coordinating committee of officials chaired by the Treasury to consider PES matters.

Public Expenditure White Paper (PEWP) *

An annual publication showing the Government's plans for public expenditure during the current and next three financial years.

Public libraries

Libraries funded by various municipal authorities for public use under the terms of the Public Libraries legislation. They provide free lending and referral services, though some services are priced.

Public Purchasing Initiative (PPI)

The initiative launched in 1980 to encourage Government (and other public sector) purchasers to develop relationships with suppliers which will assist them in improving their competitive performance.

Public Sector Borrowing Requirement (PSBR) *

A measures of the public sector's need for finance from other sectors. PSBR includes the borrowing of central government, local authorities, nationalized industries and other public corporations, but nets out intra-public-sector borrowing.

Purchase order form

A preprinted form used to enter into an agreement with a supplier, and usually including the buyer's terms and conditions.

Purchase requisition form

A preprinted form usually completed by the end-user and budget holder, requesting the buyer to make a purchase and providing authority to commit expenditure.

Purchasing Activity Review (PAR)

The formal study of a specific area of purchasing designed to identify any scope for improved value for money.

Quality control

See **Quality systems**.

Quality costs

Used to describe the costs of quality assurance and the cost to the user of non-quality, ie the cost of delivered goods which fail to perform to specification.

Quality systems

Those parts of the management systems of both supplier and purchaser which are directed towards ensuring that goods or services will be fit for their purpose.

Quote/quotation

Another term for the offer from a supplier in response to the buyer's enquiry or invitation to tender.

Rate Support Grant (RSG) ★

The general grant from central government to local authorities to supplement income from the rates/council tax.

Reading the Future: the Public Libraries Review

A review published by the Conservative government in February 1997 setting out plans for public libraries, addressing in particular issues such as the use of IT and training, and setting out the need for public library plans.

Receipts

Money coming into the organization.

Reserve ★

An amount, unallocated at first, consisting of the total of Public Expenditure for a given year which is intended to cover unforeseen items of expenditure and which cannot be properly quantified at the time of publication of the PEWP.

Resource accounting and budgeting (RAB)

A system of accounting, being introduced in government progressively from 1998 (for accounting) and 2000 (for budgeting). It focuses on resources used as well as cash spent and is based on an accruals system similar to that used in the private sector. For further information see: House of Commons Library Research Paper 99/97, available at: **http://www.parliament.uk/commons/lib/rp99/rp99-097.pdf**

Resources

Those items which an organization needs to produce goods or services, eg staff and skills, materials, premises or cash.

Resource management

Control of the items essential to an organization. These range from staff and skills through to premises, materials and cash (see also **Just-in-time**).

Revenue

Money earned and coming into the organization.

Revised estimate

A revised estimate is submitted when it becomes necessary to reduce or reallocate a Vote for which a main Supply Estimate has been presented.

Running costs

Can include various items such as materials and supplies, telephones, stationery – ie the expenditure of a department's pay bill and administrative costs.

Section *

A group of subheads in the same Vote, generally classified to the same functional category in the PEWP and the Vote Summary.

Senior management costs

In some organizations a percentage of the cost of senior management is added to the department/section costs.

Service plan

A statement to your users and management of what the information service (IS) or learning resource centre (LRC) is going to achieve in forthcoming years. Your plan could cover two to three years.

Single tendering

Inviting only one supplier or contractor to tender. If the estimated value exceeds the relevant threshold, single tendering is only permissible under the EC Supplies and Works Directives in certain situations.

SMART

Specific, Measurable, Achievable, Realistic and Timebound. A management term.

Special Libraries and Information Services (SLIS)

Usually libraries in the private sector in industrial and commercial organizations and funded by a parent organization. Government SLIS are funded by the respective department or agency.

Specification

The formal description in objective and measurable terms of the characteristics of the goods or services required.

Staff costs

Wages and salaries, including overtime and pay-related allowances, bonus payments, and National Insurance contributions. Some organizations also include training, travel and subsistence costs.

Standards

Shorthand for standard specifications – ie those established by national, European or international standards-making bodies.

Subhead *

Expenditure within a Vote which is separately identified in estimates and the Appropriation Account.

Subprogrammes *

A subdivision of the functional programmes in the Public Expenditure Surveys.

Subsidy *

A grant (ie an unrequited payment) to a producer or trader which is deemed to benefit the consumer by reducing the selling price of the products. See also **Grants**.

Supplementary Estimate *

A Supplementary Estimate is presented to Parliament during the course of the year to obtain extra money either for a new service or to make good inadequacies in existing services.

Supplier appraisal

Also known as supplier assessment or evaluation, or vendor appraisal/assessment/evaluation, this is the process of establishing whether a supplier is capable in all key respects of providing the goods and services required.

Supply Estimate *

A statement presented to the House of Commons of the estimated expenditure of a department during a financial year (ie 1 April to 31 March) asking for the necessary funds to be voted.

Supply Expenditure ★

Expenditure by central government which is financed by monies voted by Parliament in the Supply Estimates.

Tender

Another term for the supplier's bid in response to the buyer's enquiry or invitation to tender.

Tendering competition

A means by which to test and evaluate the potential suppliers to ensure a satisfactory level of service or that a product is being costed effectively.

Token subhead ★

In some cases receipts of a kind that could be Appropriations in Aid of the Vote are expected on a scale equal to or greater than the expected gross expenditure. In these circumstances, sufficient of expected receipts are shown as Appropriations in Aid to leave only a nominal balance to be voted as Supply. The Supply Estimate shows the balance of receipts expected which are payable to the Consolidated Fund as extra receipts (see above). In addition, a Supplementary Estimate for a token sum may be presented, for example, to transfer some existing provision to a new service in the same or another Vote.

Trade list

See **Approved list**. The term may also be used to describe an index of suppliers prepared by a trade association or other body, sometimes on a subscription basis.

Training budget

A specific allocation of a main budget to the cost of training and retraining staff.

Travel and subsistence budget

A specific allocation to travelling costs which may be incurred by staff carrying out their duties, or needed when staff are sent to training courses outside the organization.

Trends

A multipurpose term used by economists to interpret statistics, by academics to describe what is happening/about to happen, and by service providers to justify bids for more funds.

Turnkey contracts

Most commonly used in the context of capital projects to describe an arrangement whereby the contractor provides everything required for full operation of the facility.

Value or added value

Extra service content or improved performance brought to the task, or value added in hand which will benefit the customer/service (and will give the producer/supplier a competitive edge).

Value analysis

The breakdown of a price into its constituent cost elements (eg labour, materials, administration, distribution, profit) to identify opportunities for reduction and/or a more cost effective mix of resource inputs.

Vendor rating

A form of supplier appraisal. A technique that awards 'marks' for a supplier's actual performance on a contract against a list of significant aspects, with the supplier's 'scores' on the various aspects totalled to give a broad indicator of overall performance. Aspects of performance critical to the buyer may also be weighted to stress their importance.

Virement

Transfer of savings on one subhead to meet excess expenditure on another subhead within the same Vote.

Vote on account

Monies granted by Parliament to carry on public services from 1 April of the next financial year until Parliament has approved that year's money via the Appropriation Act, which authorizes the issue of the amount required for the full year.

Warranty

A contractual undertaking to provide a specified level of product or service support.

Work planning

Once the structure of a business has been established, work planning will detail all aspects, including financial plans.

Index